Reclaim Liberty

3–Step Plan for Restoring Our Constitutional Government

Robert J. Thorpe

Including:

The Constitution of the United States
The Declaration of Independence
The Bill of Rights and
All the Amendments

Veritas Communications, Inc.

www.VeritasIncorporated.com

For information about special discounts for bulk purchases or to schedule author interviews or other public relations events, please call:
(951) 587–1135 or (719) 275–7775
or email us at:
info@VeritasIncorporated.com

www.ReclaimLiberty.us

Manufactured in the United States of America

ISBN 978–0–6153–8044–5

Library of Congress Control Number: 2010908085

Table of Contents

Dedication

Reclaim Liberty is dedicated to my wonderful wife Donna, my children Elizabeth and Robert; to my mother–in–law Ruth; to my late father and mother Jack and Mary, and to my brothers and sisters, Don, Linda, Roberta and Jack. To my editorial and spiritual mentor and mountain climbing buddy Don Otis. To my good friends the Kotaliks, the Armstrongs, the Erferts; the Baldwins, the Zooks, Bob Pierce, Lance Hall and the Mathias'. To my church pastors Richard and Maggie Taylor; and to all my other family and friends who have helped mold me into the person I am today, thank you.

Additionally, I cannot forget the tireless efforts of our brave military, the pro–Constitutional and Tea Party patriots, our nation's honorable fiscally conservative pro–Constitutional political leaders, and those reporters, news commentators and news organizations who uphold the truth and love our country.

About the Author

Robert J. Thorpe is a fiscally conservative, pro–Constitutional author, inventor, entrepreneur and lecturer who shares our Founding Father's Constitutional vision of a small, ethical, limited government that fosters self–reliance in its citizens, not dependency and handouts. Over the years, Thorpe has worked for Walt Disney, Price Waterhouse accounting firm, the aerospace and software industries and taught at UCLA Extension. Bob has invented and filed a number of trademarks, copyrights and a patent. Thorpe is an active member of his church and his community and has volunteered a great deal of his time assisting local charities, the community fire and emergency medical services, tutoring elementary school children and attending Tea Parties. Thorpe loves the outdoors, is a skilled woodsman and has climbed numerous mountains including Mt. Whitney (14,505′) twice and the Popocatepetl volcano in Mexico (17,887′). Thorpe and his wife recently designed and built their ultra energy efficient solar / sustainable home.

Throughout this handbook are wonderful quotes from our founding fathers, great leaders and thinkers. This inspirational quote from Abraham Lincoln certainly sums up Thorpe's life

"I have an irrepressible desire to live till I can be assured that the world is a little better for my having lived in it."

Introduction – Reclaim Liberty

> *"Proclaim LIBERTY throughout all the Land unto all the Inhabitants thereof, Lev. XXV X"* — the Bible verse cast into our original Liberty Bell

Thank you for purchasing *Reclaim Liberty*. I hope this handbook will inspire and help you take personal action in helping to restore our Constitutional Republic, as our founding fathers envisioned it.

Important: I need to make it perfectly clear that I do not condone violence, only the peaceful repair of our current federal government. The Tea party and other pro–Constitutional movements are about restoration, not revolution. Our founders provided us with all the tools we need to reclaim our liberties and restore our Constitutional republic. But the participation of our citizens, actively engaged in their government, has been missing for so many years. It is time for our complacency to end and for our voices to be heard once again in Washington. Our silence has been deafening.

By no means can this handbook cover all that is wrong in Washington, but it will illustrate some of the many problems our nation is currently facing.

Why did I write *Reclaim Liberty?* It is my solemn hope that this handbook will help you become organized and will inspire you to become an active, engaged American patriot. To quote the 1980 Blues Brothers movie *"We're on a mission from God."*

In addition to my writings and observations, I have included numerous references and excerpts of books and news stories from some of our foremost political observers and writers, in order to further your understanding of today's political state. I have also included numerous quotes from our founding fathers, great thinkers, leaders and others, especially concerning liberty and tyranny. Thoughtfully evaluate and consider the many observations, ideas and arguments that are presented in this handbook. And the wisdom and reasoning found within our founder's words when determining what kind of government we currently have and truly need. Then, make up your own mind and carefully consider what role you will have in bringing needed changes to pass.

Important Definitions

- **Reclaim**: Selecting a book title is difficult, but the words 'Reclaim Liberty' are exactly what this handbook is about and what the Tea Party and other pro–Constitutional movements embrace. Here are some definitions of 'Reclaim': to get again in one's possession (we took back America); to make better in behavior or character (we reformed our leaders into a Constitutional government); to obtain a raw material by separating it from a by–product or waste (by using the white–hot fires of the Constitution, we purified Liberty as we refined the Tyranny out of Washington); bring, lead, or force to abandon a wrong or evil course of life, conduct, and adopt a right one (we forced government to use our moneys wisely and abide by the will of the people); make useful again, transform from a useless or uncultivated state (with a restored Constitutional government, the world once again saw America as a great and noble leader.)
- **Liberty**: the quality or state of being free; the power to do as one pleases; freedom from physical restraint; freedom from arbitrary or despotic control; the positive enjoyment of various social, political, or economic rights and privileges; the power of choice.
- **Tyranny**: oppressive power exerted by government (the tyranny of a police state); a government in which absolute

power is vested in a single ruler; the office, authority, and administration of a tyrant; a rigorous condition imposed by some outside agency or force.

- **Progressive Movement**: The progressive movement has been referred to as the roots of modern liberalism and the era of big government, especially with reference to its beginnings during the presidential terms of Teddy Roosevelt and Woodrow Wilson. The progressive movement can be seen as being opposed to the Constitutional views of a limited, small federal government with little intrusion into people's lives. Instead, the progressives see government as the provider of everything that the people need, or what it decides they need – in other words, an institutionalized government–state.

- **Tea Party Movement**: The Tea Party is made up of fiscally conservative, pro–Constitutional citizens, of which many claim they have never participated in politics before. Politically, they are typically (in this order) Independents, Libertarians, Republicans and Democrats. They want a small federal government, an end to the national debt, a balanced budget, are against Cap–and–Trade, want a repeal of ObamaCare and want honesty and integrity from government officials. Many Tea Party members are disenchanted with the major political parties. The idea for the Tea Party is attributed to CNBC business commentator Rick Santelli, who was outraged by the Stimulus Plan and called for a new tea party. Dubbed as 'the rant heard round the world,' Santelli went on to say that he wanted to *dump derivative securities into Lake Michigan*, and *what the country was doing must be making Benjamin Franklin and Thomas Jefferson roll over in their graves.* The Tea Party is a true grass–roots movement that was started by a young conservative mom, Keli Carender of Seattle, Washington, when she asked some of her friends from across the country to hold backyard tax day barbeques. Nationally, there are now over 2,300 Tea Party groups with about 18 million members. At present, the Tea Party doesn't have a formal political structure or have specific national leaders.

- **$1 Trillion Dollars**: A $1 dollar bill is .0043 inches thick; a stack of one trillion $1 dollar bills would be as tall as 8 ½ planet Earths stacked on top of each other. $1 million is one thousand $1,000 bills. $1 billion is one thousand $1,000,000 bills. $1 trillion is one thousand $1,000,000,000 bills. A trillion dollars is a million million or a thousand billion. You write $1 trillion dollars with a 1 followed by 12 zeros: $1,000,000,000,000, which, by the way, is the amount of money our government is currently borrowing (our budget deficit which adds to our national debt) each year for the next 10 years, in your name.

Please forget about the R's and D's. Understand that this handbook does not refer to the many problems our nation is currently facing as either Republican or Democratic problems. It's referring to American problems. During the history of America, government officials from all parties, and even the Supreme Court, have failed us by straying from the Constitutional mandates, restraints and expectations established by our founding fathers.

How this Handbook is Organized

In the front of this handbook are *3 Simple Steps for Taking Back America* and pages to write the names and contact information for your fellow patriots and upcoming events. There are also places to write the names and contact information for your representatives and for the media and to list when, how and why you contacted them, and the outcome. This is an important part of Reclaim Liberty, a call to action, or as Thomas Paine said *"Those who expect to reap the blessings of freedom must, like men, undergo the fatigue of supporting it."*

This is work that may cause you to leave your comfort zone. Our republic cannot survive unless American citizens, American patriots, support it by demanding liberty and justice for all, just as it's written in our Pledge:

"I Pledge Allegiance to the Flag
of the United States of America,
and to the Republic for which it Stands,
One Nation, under God, Indivisible,
with Liberty and Justice for All."

Becoming a politically active patriot will take time and effort. Our federal government will never rehabilitate itself willingly, and it will never truly listen to the voices and will of the American people until our voices become deafening, and our demands become relentless.

Also included in the first 3 chapters is *The Patriot's Pledge* and suggestions for when you attend pro–Constitutional meetings and rallies.

Chapters 4 – 8 contain foundational information to educate and inspire you about our nation, the founding of our country, the importance of religious faith in our founding, and your commitment as a patriot. Please read:

- *Is America a Democracy or a Republic?*
- *The Faith of our Founders*
- *What some groups believe: The 9.12 Project and The Contract from America*
- *PRLP – The Paul Revere Liberty Project*
- *The NEXT Declaration of Independence*
- *Who are WE THE PEOPLE?*

Chapter 9, *Give Me Liberty, or Give Me Debt?*, sites current books, websites and news stories and contains observations, arguments and quotes about the many problems found within our government today.

Chapters 10 and 11, *Take Back Our Government Now* and *How to Amend the U.S. Constitution* will provide commonsense ideas for fixing our government, including the possible use of states–sponsored amendments to the U.S. Constitution.

Chapters 12 and 13 lists numerous quotes from our founding fathers, our great leaders and from great thinkers, and patriotic songs including a brand new song that I wrote, *The Battle Hymn to Reclaim Liberty.* I hope they inspire you as much as they have inspired me.

The remainder of this handbook contains some of the most important documents I could include: *The Declaration of Independence, The Bill of Rights, The Constitution of the United States, and the amendments*. The text of these documents was taken directly from the U.S. Archives website. Read, reread and highlight these important documents, which are the foundation of our republic. It is due to the fact that government officials have been ignoring these important documents for so many years, that your becoming an active outspoken patriot and this handbook are both important.

In addition to these important U.S. documents, I encourage you to learn everything you can about the lives and writings of our founding fathers, our great leaders and the founding of our nation. A very good place to start is Dr. Jonathan Mott's website:

www.thisnation.com

Books You Should also Read:

- *The Five Thousand Year Leap,* by W. Cleon Skousen, James Michael Pratt, Carlos L Packard, and Evan Frederickson
- *A Patriot's History of the United States,* by Larry Schweikart and Michael Allen
- *American Progressivism,* by Ronald J. Pestritto
- *New Deal or Raw Deal?: How FDR's Economic Legacy Has Damaged America,* by Burton W. Folsom
- *Samuel Adams, A Life,* by Ira Stoll
- *The Real George Washington* (American Classic Series), by Jay A. Parry
- *The Real Thomas Jefferson* (American Classic Series), by Andrew M. Allison
- *The Real Benjamin Franklin* (American Classic Series), by Andrew M. Allison
- *Who Killed the Constitution?,by* Thomas E. Woods Jr. and Kevin R. C. Gutzman

- *Setting the Record Straight: American History in Black & White,* by David Barton
- *The Road to Serfdom: Text and Documents—The Definitive Edition* (The Collected Works of F. A. Hayek) (Volume 2), by F. A. Hayek
- Books by: Newt Gingrich, Glenn Beck, Sean Hannity, and Bill O'Reilly
- *Confessions of a Black Conservative,* by Lloyd Marcus

News Websites that I Read Daily and Highly Recommend:

www.realclearpolitics.com

www.foxnews.com

www.drudgereport.com

www.nationalreview.com

www.weeklystandard.com

planetgore.nationalreview.com

I use a terrific, time saving organizational software tool for quickly reading just the headlines from the above websites (and other websites that use RSS), where you then can selectively choose and click–on and read the entire stories of interest. It's a free software product named *FeedDemon,* which can be downloaded from:

www.newsgator.com/individuals/feeddemon

Other Websites You Should Use / Visit:

www.ReclaimLiberty.us

www.thisnation.com/

www.u–s–history.com/pages/h1261.html

www.foundingfathers.info/federalistpapers

www.archives.gov

www.usconstitution.net

www.law.ou.edu/ushistory/index.shtml#1700

www.USdebtclock.org

www.the912project.com

contractfromamerica.com

www.teapartyexpress.org

www.teapartypatriots.org

taxdayteaparty.com

www.whitehouse.gov

www.senate.gov

www.house.gov

bioguide.congress.gov/biosearch/biosearch.asp

www.law.cornell.edu

www.crewsmostcorrupt.org

www.libertybellmuseum.com

You can also use a web browser to do an online search for local pro–Constitutional groups and upcoming events. For example, if you live in Denver, search:

tax day protest Denver

On the evening of April 18, 1775, Dr. Joseph Warren instructed Paul Revere to ride to Lexington, Massachusetts in order to warn Samuel Adams and John Hancock that British troops were on the march, bringing tyranny from across the ocean. Once again, 235 years later, our nation is in perilous trouble, but this time, the tyranny is from within. Who will leave the comfort of their warm beds to face the darkness and rising tide?

It's Time for You to Choose, Either:

- A nanny–state of unquenchable government power, growth, control and debt, or
- Unfettered Personal Liberty

When freedom is fleeting, liberty becomes more precious. Our nation needs you more than ever. God speed to you in these endeavors, and may God bless America and help us Reclaim Liberty!

I — 3 Simple Steps for Taking Back America

1) Study: read and learn everything you can about our country:

- The Declaration of Independence
- The Bill of Rights
- The U.S. Constitution and the Amendments

Also, learn all you can about the lives of our founding fathers and the founding and history of our nation

2) As an Individual:

- Get organized: start contacting your representatives and the media and voice your concerns
- Attend pro–Constitutional meetings, rallies and marches
- Get to know like–minded patriots and make your voice heard. Remember: the squeaky wheels get the grease

3) As a Member of a Pro–Constitutional Group(s):

- Join one or more pro–Constitution political groups
- Get organized: create petition drives and champion local and state ballot propositions to improve our government
- Lobby your state governments to call for a Constitutional Congress to pass new amendments to the U.S. Constitution
- Champion and support good, noble, honorable, ethical, honest and fiscally conservative judges and candidates
- Keep the energy and momentum going. No matter who's in power, they need persistent reminding that 'the people who constitute a nation are the source of all authority'
- Support and attend the *Paul Revere Liberty Project*

II — Patriot's Call to Action

The Patriot's Pledge

I ______________________ on ____________ pledge my allegiance to my family, my community and to the United States of America. I do solemnly swear to protect, preserve, support and defend our Constitution against all enemies, foreign and domestic, and that I will bear true faith and allegiance to the same. I promise to live truthfully, honorably and ethically and to demand the same from my government. I promise to confront and expose injustice and tyranny while demanding liberty, and a limited, representative, accountable, honest, ethical, transparent, sovereign and solvent government. And to affirm these promises, I pledge to my fellow American patriots my Life, my Fortune and my Sacred Honor.

Your comments and commitments:

____

____

____

____

____

____

____

____

Use the following pages as a reference for:

- Contacting fellow patriots
- Attending meetings and events
- Contacting your local, state and federal representatives
- Contacting the White House
- Contacting the Media.

When contacting your representatives, you will need to list on the following pages when, how, who and why you contacted them, and the outcome. This is an important part of this handbook for reclaiming and repairing our government. Call them on the telephone and mail letters (old school) in addition to email and electronic communications.

Do not rely solely upon electronic communications because they can be easily filtered, ignored and deleted. As a matter of fact, it's difficult to even locate a direct email address for most representatives, and even when they email you, replying to their email typically doesn't even work. Is this their idea of a 'representative' government? This makes direct communication, letters and telephone calls, even more important.

When communicating, be passionate and determined, but it's very important that you're also respectful and polite.

Your List of Patriotic Heroes

Name	Contact Information

List of Patriotic Heroes

Name	Contact Information

Upcoming Meetings and Events

Date & Time	
Event	
Contact Info	
What to Bring	
Notes	
Date & Time	
Event	
Contact Info	
What to Bring	
Notes	
Date & Time	
Event	
Contact Info	
What to Bring	
Notes	
Date & Time	
Event	
Contact Info	
What to Bring	
Notes	

Upcoming Meetings and Events

Date & Time	
Event	
Contact Info	
What to Bring	
Notes	
Date & Time	
Event	
Contact Info	
What to Bring	
Notes	
Date & Time	
Event	
Contact Info	
What to Bring	
Notes	
Date & Time	
Event	
Contact Info	
What to Bring	
Notes	

Upcoming Meetings and Events

Date & Time	
Event	
Contact Info	
What to Bring	
Notes	
Date & Time	
Event	
Contact Info	
What to Bring	
Notes	
Date & Time	
Event	
Contact Info	
What to Bring	
Notes	
Date & Time	
Event	
Contact Info	
What to Bring	
Notes	

Upcoming Meetings and Events

Date & Time	
Event	
Contact Info	
What to Bring	
Notes	
Date & Time	
Event	
Contact Info	
What to Bring	
Notes	
Date & Time	
Event	
Contact Info	
What to Bring	
Notes	
Date & Time	
Event	
Contact Info	
What to Bring	
Notes	

Contacting Local and State Representatives

Date & Time	
Who Contacted	
Contact Info	
What Outcome	
Notes	
Date & Time	
Who Contacted	
Contact Info	
What Outcome	
Notes	
Date & Time	
Who Contacted	
Contact Info	
What Outcome	
Notes	
Date & Time	
Who Contacted	
Contact Info	
What Outcome	
Notes	

Contacting Local and State Representatives

Date & Time	
Who Contacted	
Contact Info	
What Outcome	
Notes	
Date & Time	
Who Contacted	
Contact Info	
What Outcome	
Notes	
Date & Time	
Who Contacted	
Contact Info	
What Outcome	
Notes	
Date & Time	
Who Contacted	
Contact Info	
What Outcome	
Notes	

Contacting Local and State Representatives

Date & Time	
Who Contacted	
Contact Info	
What Outcome	
Notes	
Date & Time	
Who Contacted	
Contact Info	
What Outcome	
Notes	
Date & Time	
Who Contacted	
Contact Info	
What Outcome	
Notes	
Date & Time	
Who Contacted	
Contact Info	
What Outcome	
Notes	

Contacting Local and State Representatives

Date & Time	
Who Contacted	
Contact Info	
What Outcome	
Notes	
Date & Time	
Who Contacted	
Contact Info	
What Outcome	
Notes	
Date & Time	
Who Contacted	
Contact Info	
What Outcome	
Notes	
Date & Time	
Who Contacted	
Contact Info	
What Outcome	
Notes	

Contacting Federal Representatives
U.S. Senate and House of Representatives
E Capitol St NE and 1st St NE, Washington, DC 20001
(202) 224–3121 Switchboard
www.senate.gov www.house.gov

Date & Time	
Who Contacted	
Contact Info	
What Outcome	
Notes	
Date & Time	
Who Contacted	
Contact Info	
What Outcome	
Notes	
Date & Time	
Who Contacted	
Contact Info	
What Outcome	
Notes	
Date & Time	
Who Contacted	
Contact Info	
What Outcome	

Contacting Federal Representatives

Date & Time	
Who Contacted	
Contact Info	
What Outcome	
Notes	
Date & Time	
Who Contacted	
Contact Info	
What Outcome	
Notes	
Date & Time	
Who Contacted	
Contact Info	
What Outcome	
Notes	
Date & Time	
Who Contacted	
Contact Info	
What Outcome	
Notes	

Contacting Federal Representatives

Date & Time	
Who Contacted	
Contact Info	
What Outcome	
Notes	
Date & Time	
Who Contacted	
Contact Info	
What Outcome	
Notes	
Date & Time	
Who Contacted	
Contact Info	
What Outcome	
Notes	
Date & Time	
Who Contacted	
Contact Info	
What Outcome	
Notes	

Contacting Federal Representatives

Date & Time	
Who Contacted	
Contact Info	
What Outcome	
Notes	
Date & Time	
Who Contacted	
Contact Info	
What Outcome	
Notes	
Date & Time	
Who Contacted	
Contact Info	
What Outcome	
Notes	
Date & Time	
Who Contacted	
Contact Info	
What Outcome	
Notes	

Contacting The White House

1600 Pennsylvania Avenue NW Washington, DC 20500
202–456–1111 Comments
202–456–1414 Switchboard
202–456–2461 FAX www.whitehouse.gov/contact

Date & Time	
Who Contacted	
Contact Info	
What Outcome	
Notes	
Date & Time	
Who Contacted	
Contact Info	
What Outcome	
Notes	
Date & Time	
Who Contacted	
Contact Info	
What Outcome	
Notes	
Date & Time	
Who Contacted	
Contact Info	
What Outcome	

Contacting The White House

Date & Time	
Who Contacted	
Contact Info	
What Outcome	
Notes	
Date & Time	
Who Contacted	
Contact Info	
What Outcome	
Notes	
Date & Time	
Who Contacted	
Contact Info	
What Outcome	
Notes	
Date & Time	
Who Contacted	
Contact Info	
What Outcome	
Notes	

Contacting The White House

Date & Time	
Who Contacted	
Contact Info	
What Outcome	
Notes	
Date & Time	
Who Contacted	
Contact Info	
What Outcome	
Notes	
Date & Time	
Who Contacted	
Contact Info	
What Outcome	
Notes	
Date & Time	
Who Contacted	
Contact Info	
What Outcome	
Notes	

Contacting The White House

Date & Time	
Who Contacted	
Contact Info	
What Outcome	
Notes	
Date & Time	
Who Contacted	
Contact Info	
What Outcome	
Notes	
Date & Time	
Who Contacted	
Contact Info	
What Outcome	
Notes	
Date & Time	
Who Contacted	
Contact Info	
What Outcome	
Notes	

Contacting The Media

Date & Time	
Who Contacted	
Contact Info	
What Outcome	
Notes	
Date & Time	
Who Contacted	
Contact Info	
What Outcome	
Notes	
Date & Time	
Who Contacted	
Contact Info	
What Outcome	
Notes	
Date & Time	
Who Contacted	
Contact Info	
What Outcome	
Notes	

Contacting The Media

Date & Time	
Who Contacted	
Contact Info	
What Outcome	
Notes	
Date & Time	
Who Contacted	
Contact Info	
What Outcome	
Notes	
Date & Time	
Who Contacted	
Contact Info	
What Outcome	
Notes	
Date & Time	
Who Contacted	
Contact Info	
What Outcome	
Notes	

Contacting The Media

Date & Time	
Who Contacted	
Contact Info	
What Outcome	
Notes	
Date & Time	
Who Contacted	
Contact Info	
What Outcome	
Notes	
Date & Time	
Who Contacted	
Contact Info	
What Outcome	
Notes	
Date & Time	
Who Contacted	
Contact Info	
What Outcome	
Notes	

How to Write a Letter

When writing to your representatives, the media or others, be:

- Polite
- Passionate
- Professional
- Focused
- Concise (short)

If you ramble on in the letter, they wont understand the point of your letter and may simply discard it. Don't stray from the topic(s). If you're writing about high taxes, don't bring up you your right to bear arms.

No name–calling or threats. Understand that the letter will probably be opened and read by a staffer, so it is best to be polite and concise in hopes that they will not discard the letter, but instead, will pass it on up the chain of command.

Here's a sample letter:

July 4, 2010

Representative Joseph M. Snort
U.S. Hour of Representatives
E Capitol St NE and 1st St NE
Washington, DC 20001

Re: The American Clean Energy and Security Act (H.R. 2454)

Dear Representative Snort:

My family and I urge you to vote against *The American Clean Energy and Security Act* (H.R. 2454). This Cap–and–Trade bill will cause terrible financial hardship on the American people and will not improve our environment. All recent national polling shows that the American people do not support this bill by a ratio of 3 to 1 against it.

During one of our worst economic downturns in recent history, congress needs to focus its energies on creating jobs in the private sector, not on expensive legislation for addressing the unproven 'theory' of global warming.

Respectfully yours,

Mr. Dan Patriot
123 First Street
Anytown, NY, 99999–9999

III — Before You go to a Rally

In the April 19, 2010 Real Clear Politics story, *Tea Partiers Fight Culture of Dependence,* Michael Barone describes an April 15, 2009 Tea Party rally where a provocative TV reporter, CNN's Susan Roesgen, tries to confuse and demean a Tea Party protester by telling him about all the financial benefits he and his state get from the federal government.

Please understand that your behavior is being observed by those who might want to harm the pro–Constitutional movements, and also by those who may want to join. How you behave, what you say, what you write on your signs or wear on your body may help or may tarnish thousands of other patriots, and harm the success of the movements.

> *"I hope that I shall always possess firmness and virtue enough to maintain what I consider to be the most enviable of all titles, the character of an honest man." — George Washington*

Display the Truth

According to an April 20, 2010 FoxNews.com story, *Tea Partiers Seek 'Teachable Moment,' Not Oregon Teacher's Job,* Jana Winter writes

> The Oregon Tea Party doesn't want to see middle school teacher Jason Levin fired, even though he has publicly denounced them as a bunch of *"racists, homophobes and morons."*
>
> Levin declared his mission to 'dismantle and demolish' the Tea Party on his 'Crash the Tea Party' website. In recent weeks, Levin announced his intention to embarrass Tea Partiers by attending their rallies dressed as Adolf Hitler, carrying signs bearing racist, sexist and anti–gay epithets and acting as offensively as possible —

anything, he said, short of throwing punches. In an interview, Levin said, *"Our goal is that whenever a Tea Partier says 'Barack Obama was not born in America,' we're going be right there next to them saying, 'Yeah, in fact he wasn't born on Earth. He's an alien.'"*

And in a now deleted website post, Levin called on his supporters to collect the Social Security numbers — among other personal identifying information — about as many Tea Party supporters as possible. *"The more data we can mine from the Tea Partiers, the more mayhem we can cause with it..."* he wrote.

With this in mind, you need to understand whom you're up against and make certain you understand the facts (truth) behind the issues. Also make sure that you do not mistake political speech or exaggeration, for fact. The term 'death panel' makes a terrific sound–bite for Sarah Palin, but is more speculation than fact. Focusing on the alleged controversy over Obama's birth certificate is a distraction and does the movement more harm than good. The left–wing media would love to show a video of you talking about death panels or show a picture of you holding up a sign about the president's missing birth certificate. They will use these images to paint all the pro–Constitutional patriots with a broad brush and ridicule and dismiss you and the movements, which does a disservice to your fellow patriots. Know and present the facts so that your passion and ideas are not dismissed because of misinformation.

In addition, do not be biased or dishonest. Don't put references to communists or the Nazis (i.e., calling Obama a Nazi) or have anything on a sign that might suggest racism, or threats of violence towards others. These will all be used against you by the left–wing media and will harm the success of the movements.

Be appropriate, knowledgeable, truthful, patriotic and energetic.

Your Appearance

Wear patriotic clothes (if you have them). Dress nicely, but please don't show up at a rally with a 9 mm pistol on your hip. I love owning and shooting target pistols and my skeet shotgun, but I don't need to parade my firearms around a rally that's called to protest high taxes. Once again, the left–wing media would simply love to show a video of you with a gun at a rally in order to cast you as someone to be feared and not trusted, which does a disservice to you and your fellow patriots. Also, we want the local police and government officials to condone, perhaps even support the rallies. Causing an officer to wonder about your gun–carrying intentions certainly doesn't help his day or the cause.

> *"The great consolation in life is to say what one thinks."* — *Voltaire*

Confrontations

You may encounter people who are protesting your event and trying to deny you of your first amendment right to free speech. According to Sir James Matthew Barrie *"Always be a little kinder than necessary."* Oftentimes, when you return anger with kindness, you will frustrate your opponent and cause them to give up and walk away. So if someone makes an angry gesture or yells something toward you, simply smile and give a friendly wave back in their direction. You kindness may even help to change their opinions of the movement.

These people want to engage you in a fight or war of words, but if you take ownership of the confrontation and don't give in to their hateful desires, it will typically frustrate them, defuse the situation and cause them to move on. If the left–wing media can catch you being confrontational, angry or vulgar, they will use it to demean you, the movement and other patriots. Set a positive, friendly example for others to follow.

Present a knowledgeable, tolerant, passionate, polite, friendly demeanor both at the rally and elsewhere, especially with your friends, relatives, co–workers, strangers and the media. Clap, cheer, sing, and wave flags and homemade signs. Have fun and enjoy spending time with your fellow patriots.

Stay Focused

Whether you're at a rally, a Tea Party meeting or simply having a frank discussion with friends, stay focused on big picture issues and the most important problems that need to be addressed, specifically those that 'can' be accomplished. It is extremely easy to get side tracked onto the numerous smaller problems and injustices that are occurring or have occurred during our nation's history.

These smaller problems can be personal 'pet–peeves', issues that you are personally concerned and passionate about, such as the indoctrination of school students, the legality of income taxes or the loss of our monetary gold standard. These diversions can eat up valuable time during a meeting, cannot be easily solved and may have a tendency to strain the patience of some of the attendees, your fellow patriots. Choose your battles wisely, those that can be fought and won. Stay focused and consistent in where you place your energies and passions.

IV — Is America a Democracy or a Republic?

The following text was researched and written by Jonathan Mott, Ph.D. and can be found at:

www.thisnation.com/textbook/constitution–features.html

A Republican Form of Government

One of the most widely held misconceptions about the American system of government is that it is a democracy. In reality, the American framers were suspicious of democracy and the problems that attended it. In a pure democracy, the people vote directly on every major political question, with the majority determining which course to take. Because there is nothing to prevent the majority from taking the property, liberty or even the lives of the minority in such a system, the Framers believed that democracy was just as likely to result in tyranny as was a monarchy. Indeed, (James) Madison argued, direct democracies have *"in general been as short in their lives as they have been violent in their deaths"* (Federalist No. 10).

Properly understood, the form of government established by the Constitution is not a democracy, but rather a republic. What is a republic? Madison offered this definition in the Federalist No. 39:

> *"We may define a republic to be, or at least may bestow that name on, a government which derives all its powers directly or indirectly from the great body of the people, and is administered by persons holding their offices during pleasure, for a limited period, or during good behavior."*

In other words, in a republic, the people elect representatives to make decisions on their behalf in the political process. In a republic, the people do not voice their opinions directly in the policy making process, but rather their views are conveyed through their representatives. Such a scheme, Madison argued, will:

> *"Refine and enlarge the public views, by passing them through the medium of a chosen body of citizens, whose wisdom may best discern the true interest of their country, and whose patriotism and love of justice will be least likely to sacrifice it to temporary or partial considerations. Under such a regulation, it may well happen that the public voice, pronounced by the representatives of the people, will be more consonant to the public good than if pronounced by the people themselves, convened for the purpose (Federalist No. 10)."*

How important was republicanism to the success of the government established by the Constitution? Madison wrote:

> *"It is evident that no other form would be reconcilable with the genius of the people of America; with the fundamental principles of the Revolution; or with that honorable determination which animates every votary of freedom, to rest all our political experiments on the capacity of mankind for self–government. If the plan of the convention, therefore, be found to depart from the republican character, its advocates must abandon it as no longer defensible (see Federalist No. 39)."*

The republican form of government the Framers established is largely intact in the United States, especially at the national level. While Senators are now directly elected by the people (instead of by state legislatures) and several states have enacted provisions allowing for various forms of direct democracy (such as ballot initiatives and referendums), the American system of government is primarily a representative republic, not a democracy.

By design, then, the decisions made by America's political leaders are often different from the will of the majority of the people at any given point in time. Individual political leaders, however, are kept in check through frequent elections. Members of the House of Representatives must face reelection every two years and Senators every six. Presidents serve terms of four years. By staggering these elections so that there is never a case in which congressional seats and the presidency are being contested at the same time, it is impossible for a majority faction to take control of the national government through one election.

V — The Faith of our Founders

Our Faith and Liberties under Attack

Many of the settlers who came to America were escaping religious persecution or seeking religious freedom. Even during the late 1700's, New England still had a strong, evident Puritan heritage, which had already lasted 150 years and which continued through the founding of the United States and beyond.

According to the 2007 Pew Research Center's survey of 35,000 Americans 18 years old or older, faith is still an important component in the lives of Americans today. Of those interviewed, 78.4 percent said that they were affiliated with a Christian faith and 4.7 percent said that they were affiliated with either the Jewish, Muslim or Hindu faiths. Only 16.1 percent said that they were not affiliated with any specific faith.

Considering that over 83 percent of Americans professed faith in an established religion, it's surprising to discover that there are those within our country who are actively trying to reduce or eliminate religion and faith from public life. In fact, when you do an online search using the words 'Religious Freedom Under Attack,' you will find over 900,000 website listings.

In his 2010 book, *To Save America: Stopping Obama's Secular–Socialist Machine,* former Speaker of the House of Representatives, Newt Gingrich, refers to this trend as the 'secularization of America.' The people who are actively working to reduce the influences of religion in America are what Gingrich refers to as 'secular socialists.' In his 2007 book, *Culture Warrior,* Bill O'Reilly refers to these same people as 'secular progressives.' These secular socialists or progressives often cite the Constitutional separation of church and state as their chief argument against public displays of religion. These detractors never seem to mention that the words *separation of church and state* are nowhere to be found within the U.S. Constitution, or any of our other founding documents.

Our founders strived to safeguard America against religious oppression. Many of our early settlers left England because of the church's long history of wielding enormous influences over the government, its' policies and its' citizens. In response, our founders wrote in the first amendment of the Bill of Rights *"Congress shall make no law respecting an establishment of religion, or prohibiting the free exercise thereof."* This is not Constitutional separation of church and state. Congress is only restrained from making laws establishing a religion, or restricting citizens from participating in religious practices. It would be unconstitutional for congress to make a law that forced you to join the 'Church of USA,' or forbid you from attending a specific church or practicing your faith on a specific day of the week. Additionally, congress is not restricted by the Constitution from having an opening prayer during its sessions, establishing Christmas as a national holiday, having the words 'one nation under God' in our Pledge of Allegiance, or even printing 'In God we Trust' on our currency. But all four of these examples have been targets of anti–religion groups.

The American Civil Liberties Union (ACLU) is groundless when it cites separation of church and state when threatening to sue a city for allowing a Nativity Scene or a Menorah, or both, to be displayed on public property. These threats are nothing more than strong–arm legal tactics, which typically work. Many cities lack the political will or cannot afford the costly litigation to defend themselves, and simply give–in in order to avoid the threatened legal action. Consider the language in the Bill of Rights *'Congress' shall make no law...* When a city, a public school, or any other non–congressional public organization chooses to display a religious symbol or host a religious event, their 'expression' has nothing to do with congress or any law that congress may have passed.

Our founders wrote in the tenth amendment of the Bill of Rights *"The powers not delegated to the United States by the Constitution, nor prohibited by it to the States, are reserved to the States respectively, or to the people."* The Constitution does not prohibit the states or the people from expressing their religious beliefs in the public square, but instead, it protects those rights of expression.

And according to the tenth amendment, the Constitution does forbid the states from passing laws that congress is also restrained from enacting, in other words, neither congress nor the states can pass laws that restrain public expressions of religion. But by impeding our protected religious freedoms, the actions of the ACLU and others have nothing to do with the Constitution, but they do have a direct impact on us by reducing our personal, protected liberties.

Americans have a rich, historic heritage of religious freedom and faith. But some in our society, like the ACLU, the People for the American Way and others, are actively trying to secularize America by making it 'politically incorrect' to display and celebrate our religious beliefs and traditions in public. They have even resorted to costly court actions against those with whom they disagree. Even worse, physical attacks have been made against houses of worship, the clergy and their congregations.

A Nation Founded on Faith

It's important to understand what faith is and the significance and impact that religious faith played in the founding and development of our nation. Faith is a quality that many feel improves both the individual and their community. People of faith are typically less self–centered, have a broader, more outward and hopeful view of life, and are more likely to be law abiding. People of faith typically have greater empathy towards others, which can be seen in charitable acts towards the poor and a heightened concern for their fellow man. Faith also causes people to become better stewards of their country and communities, when those things are viewed as ordained or gifted from God.

In comparison to other nations, America has a long history of being extremely generous when helping poorer nations and responding to natural disasters. In the aftermath of the January 2010 earthquake in Haiti, the American government, our private relief organizations and contributions from individuals surpassed every other nation in providing manpower, materials and financial assistance to the Haitian people.

Some of America's greatest sacrifices have come during times of war. During World War II (1941–1945), almost 1.08 million Americans were killed or wounded with a cost of about $4.7 trillion (in today's dollars) while trying to liberate numerous countries and millions of people. Below is a link to the prayer *"Let Our Hearts Be Stout"* which was written and spoken by President Franklin D. Roosevelt on the evening of June 6, 1944 (D–Day) to the nation on radio, while American, British and Canadian troops were fighting to establish five beachheads on the coast of Normandy, in northern France.

www.historyplace.com/speeches/fdr–prayer.htm

America's history is filled with examples of religious faith in our leaders and communities. In September 1777, after the Revolutionary Army had suffered repeated defeats by the British, Samuel Adams addressed the Continental Congress saying:

"Let us awaken then and evince a different spirit, a spirit that shall inspire the people with confidence in themselves and in us, a spirit that will encourage them to persevere in this glorious struggle until their rights and liberties shall be established on a rock. We have proclaimed to the world our determination to 'die freemen rather than to live slaves'. We have appealed to Heaven for the justice of our cause, and in Heaven have we placed our trust. Numerous have been the manifestations of God's providence in sustaining us. In the gloomy period of adversity, we have had 'our cloud by day and pillar of fire by night'. We have been reduced to distress and the arm of Omnipotence has raised us up. Let us still rely in humble confidence on Him who is mighty to save. Good tidings will soon arrive. We shall never be abandoned by Heaven, while we act worthy of its aid and protection."

Several weeks after Adams' address, news arrived of British General John Burgoyne's surrender at Saratoga, a pivotal battle which gave hope to the colonies and marked the beginning of our eventual victory against the British.

Adams' reference to 'our cloud by day and pillar of fire by night' is from the 13th chapter of the Old Testament book of Exodus, verses 18–22. In these verses, the Bible describes how God went before the people of Israel, leading them through the wilderness with a pillar of cloud by day and a pillar of fire by night. This reference is a strong, powerful indication of Adams' belief that the American people were ordained and protected by God, in the same way as God's 'chosen' people, the Old Testament Israelites.

In his 1894 book, *A Cloud of Witnesses,* Stephen Abbott Northrop compiled citations from over eight hundred prominent individuals from around the world, citing their personal beliefs in the Bible and in Christianity. Northrop contacted and received numerous correspondences from notable individuals about their personal beliefs and religious faith. Northrop also researched and cited the writings of those who had already died, or cited the testimonies of people who had personally known those deceased individuals.

I selected and reviewed citations from the 352 Americans documented in Northrop's book. These individuals were typically educated, successful, professional people. Many served in leadership roles in both the government and the private sector, and none of them worked for, or as, religious clergy. Many of those Americans cited had numerous, impressive careers that summarized as follows:

10 – Signers of the Declaration of Independence and the U.S. Constitution
21 – United States Presidents, including 21 of our first 23 Presidents
139 – Statesman, including Congressmen, Governors, Diplomats
13 – Supreme Court Justices
3 – Judges
47 – Lawyers
32 – Military generals and admirals, some who served in the Revolutionary and Civil Wars
4 – Other people associated with military affairs
10 – Physicians and surgeons
3 – Inventors
88 – Heads of organizations, including government institutions, associations, colleges and universities
14 – Industrialists, including heads of industry and financiers
2 – Merchants
27 – Scientists, including college and university professors

69 – Educators
16 – Journalists, including editors of major publications
34 – Authors
3 – Historians
18 – Poets
1 – Artist
15 – Philanthropists
10 – Reformers and abolitionists
8 – Explorers and travelers

Of the Americans cited, the years of their birth are as follows:

1% – were born from the 1400's–1600's
6% – were born during the years of 1700–1749
16% – were born during the years of 1750–1799
24% – were born during the years of 1800–1839
53% – were born on or around the mid 1800's

A majority of the Americans cited in Northrop's book professed a basic respect for the Bible and Christianity based upon their practical and historic contributions to society. While many also expressed a much deeper faith in their religious beliefs:

88% – professed that the Bible was inspired by God
81% – professed that Jesus Christ was Divine
51% – professed that Jesus Christ was their Savior, redeemer or their salvation

The following excerpts from *A Cloud of Witnesses* are from some of the more notable Americans and demonstrates a recurring theme of religious belief and faith. Due to their lengths, the full citations, sources and references were not included, but will be in full in my next book.

George Washington, 1732–1799, First President of the United States. *"And now, Almighty Father, if it is Thy holy will that we shall obtain a place and name among the nations of the earth, grant that we may be enabled to show our gratitude for Thy goodness by our endeavors to fear and obey Thee. Bless us with Thy wisdom in our counsels, success in battle and let all our victories be tempered with tempered humanity. Endow also our enemies with enlightened minds that they become sensible of their injustice and willing to restore our liberty and peace. Grant the petition of Thy servant for the sake of Him whom Thou hast called 'Thy beloved Son,' nevertheless, not my will, but Thine be done."*

John Adams, 1735–1826, Second President of the United States. To Thomas Jefferson *"Suppose a nation in some distant region should take the Bible for their only law book, and every member should regulate his conduct by the precepts there contained. Every member would be obliged in conscience to temperance, frugality and industry; to justice, kindness, and charity towards his fellow men, and to piety, love, and reverence toward Almighty."*

Thomas Jefferson, 1743–1826,Third President of the United States. *"A more beautiful or precious morsel of ethics I have never seen, it is a document in proof that I am a real Christian, that is to say, a disciple of the doctrines of Jesus."*

James Madison, 1751–1836, Fourth President of the United States. Among his manuscripts are minute and elaborate notes made by him on the Gospels and the Acts of the Apostles, which evince, a close and discriminating study of the Sacred Writings.

John Quincy Adams, 1767–1848, Sixth President of the United States. *"There are two prayers that I love to say; the first is the 'Lord's Prayer', and because the Lord taught it; and the other is what seems to be a child's prayer 'Now I lay me down to sleep.' But I have added a few words more to the prayer, so as to express my trust in*

Christ, and also to acknowledge what I ask for; I ask as a favor, and not because I deserve it."

Andrew Jackson, 1767–1845, Seventh President of the United States. *"The Bible is true. Upon that sacred Volume, I rest my hope of eternal salvation, through the merits of our blessed Lord and Savior, Jesus Christ."*

Martin Van Buren, 1782–1862, Eighth President of the United States. *"I only look to the gracious protection of that Divine Being, whose strengthening support I humbly solicit, and whom I fervently pray, to look down upon us all. May it be among the dispensations of His Providence, to bless our beloved country, with honors and length of days; may her ways be ways of pleasantness, and all her paths, peace."*

William Henry Harrison, 1773–1841, Ninth President of the United States. *"I deem the present occasion sufficiently important and solemn, to justify me in expressing to my fellow citizens, a profound reverence for the Christian religion, and a thorough conviction that sound morals, religious liberty and a just sense of religious responsibility, are essentially connected with all true and lasting happiness."*

John Tyler, 1790–1862, Tenth President of the United States. It was comforting to know that the great work of eternity had not been neglected. His gifted mind held fast as a foundation of its faith, and hope to the oracles of God. He was long accustomed to meditate on things of eternity. And when a few years ago, he was prostrated by sickness and the idea of approaching dissolution, the testimony of the pastor, whose services he was so fond of attending in that church he had so reverently joined, showed the brightness of the Christian faith, in which he died.

James Knox Polk, 1795–1849, Eleventh President of the United States. In his last sickness, he expressed his sense of unworthiness before God, together with painful apprehension, that he had long delayed to seek the Divine favor, and to devote himself to the service of Christ, to expect His pardoning mercy on his deathbed. He at last professed to have obtained pardon for all his sins, and the purification of his heart, through the blood of our Lord, Jesus Christ.

Zachary Taylor, 1784–1850, Twelfth President of the United States. *"It was for the love of the truths of this great Book, that our fathers abandoned their native shores for the wilderness. Animated by its lofty principles, they toiled and suffered till the desert blossomed as the rose. The same truths sustained them in their resolutions to become a free nation, and guided by the wisdom of this Book, they founded a government under which we have grown from three millions to more than twenty millions of people, and from being but a stock on the borders of this Continent, we have spread from the Atlantic to the Pacific."*

Franklin Pierce, 1804–1869, Fourteenth President of the United States. *"I should shrink from a clear duty if I failed to express my deepest conviction, that we can place no secure reliance upon any apparent progress, if it be not sustained by national integrity, resting upon the great truths affirmed and illustrated by Divine Revelation."*

James Buchanan, 1791–1868, Fifteenth President of the United States. *"I trust in God, that through the merits and atonement of His Son, we may both be prepared for the inevitable change. I ought constantly to pray: 'Help Thou my unbelief.' I trust that the Almighty Father, through the merits and atonement of His Son, will yet vouchsafe to me a clearer, and stronger faith, than I possess."*

Abraham Lincoln, 1809–1865, Sixteenth President of the United States. *"In regard to this great Book, I have only to say that it is the best gift God ever gave to man. All the good, from the Savior of the world, is communicated through this Book. But for this Book, we could not know right from wrong. All those things, desirable for man, are contained in it"*

Andrew Johnson, 1808–1875, Seventeenth President of the United States. *"I do believe in almighty God. And I believe also in the Bible. Let us look forward to the time when we can take the flag of our country and nail it below the Cross, and there, let it wave as it waved in the olden times, and let us gather around it and inscribe for our motto: 'Liberty and Union, one and inseparable, now and forever', and exclaim 'Christ first, our country next.'"*

Ulysses S. Grant, 1822–1885, General in Chief during the Civil War, Eighteenth President of the United States. *"My advice to Sunday schools, no matter what their denomination, is: 'Hold fast to the Bible, as the sheet anchor of your liberties; write its precepts in your hearts, and practice them in your lives.' To the influence of this Book, are we indebted for all the progress made in true civilization, and to this, must we look as our guide in the future. Righteousness exalteth a nation, but sin is a reproach to any people."*

Rutherford B. Hayes, 1822–1893, Nineteenth President of the United States, Major General in Civil War. *"I am a firm believer in the Divine teachings, perfect example, and atoning sacrifice of Jesus Christ. I believe also in the Holy Scriptures, as the revealed Word of God, to the world for its enlightenment and salvation."*

James A. Garfield, 1831–1881, Twentieth President of the United States. Whilst a student at Williams College, he with other students on 'Mountain Day' climbed one of the high peaks, seven miles distant. The surrounding scenery was enough to awaken religious awe. Just then, young Garfield broke the silence: *"Boys, it is a habit of mine to read a chapter in the Bible every evening with my absent mother. Shall I read aloud?"* The little company assented, and drawing from his pocket a well–worn Testament, he read in soft rich tones, the chapter which the mother in Ohio was reading at the same time, and then, called on a classmate on that mountain top to pray.

Stephen Grover Cleveland, Twenty–second President of the United States. *"All must admit, that the reception of the teachings of Christ, results in the purest patriotism in the most scrupulous fidelity, to public trust and in the best type of citizenship. Those who manage the affairs of government, are by this means reminded that the law of God demands that they should be courageously true to the interests of the people, and that the Ruler of the Universe will require of them a strict account of their stewardship. The teachings of both human and divine law, thus merging into one word 'duty,' form the only union of church and state, that a civil and religious government can recognize."*

Benjamin Harrison, Twenty–third President of the United States. *"That I am a firm believer in the religion of Jesus Christ, and the Holy Scriptures as the Word of God, is not a virtue of mine. I imbibed it at my mother's breast, and can no more divest myself of it, than I can of my nature."*

Benjamin Franklin, 1706–1790, Statesman and Philosopher. *"Here is my creed: I believe in one God, the Creator of the universe, that He governs it by His providence, that he ought to be worshipped, that the most acceptable service we can render Him is doing good to His other children, that the soul of man is immortal, and will be treated with justice in another world, respecting his conduct in this. As to Jesus of Nazareth, my opinion of whom you particularly desire, I think His system of morals and His religion as He left them to us, the best the world ever saw, or is likely to see."*

Richard Henry Lee, 1732–1794, Orator Statesman and Patriot. A committee of three consisting of Richard Henry Lee, Samuel Adams, and General Daniel Roberdeau, reported in the Congress of the Revolution, November 1, 1777, this resolution, recommending the setting apart of *"Thursday the 18th of December next, for solemn thanksgiving and praise, that with one heart and one voice, the good people may express the grateful feelings of their hearts, and consecrate themselves to the service of their Divine Benefactor; and* *that, together with their sincere acknowledgments and offerings, they may join the penitent confession of their manifold sins, whereby, they had forfeited every favor, and their humble and earnest supplication, that it may please God, through the merits of Jesus Christ, mercifully to forgive, and blot them out of remembrance."* Journal of Congress Volume III pages 467 and 468. Please note: Samuel Adams wrote the above resolution.

Ephraim Kirby Smith, 1824–1893, Confederate Major General and Educator. *"I know that my Redeemer liveth, and that He shall stand at the latter day upon the earth. Without that inestimable comfort, and undying faith, that comes from the sacred Scriptures, and the religion of Jesus Christ, life would be a miserable failure."*

H. H. Markham, Governor of California. *"Permit me to say that I am a firm believer in Christianity, and its Book. I am thoroughly convinced that all the Churches of Jesus Christ, are doing a vast amount of good, in their respective capacities."*

David Josiah Brewer, Associate Justice of the United States Supreme Court. *"I believe in Jesus Christ as the great Helper, Comforter and Savior of humanity, and the Holy Bible as bearing to us the story of his mission, the rules of duty, the revelation of Eternal Life, and also the conditions under which the attainment of that life are possible. No Book contains more truths, or is more worthy of confidence than the Bible; none brings more joy to the sorrowing, more strength to the weak, or more stimulus to the nobly ambitious; none makes life sweeter, or death easier, or less sad."*

Mark Walrod Harrington, Astronomer and Chief of Weather Bureau. *"I do not hesitate to express my extreme admiration for the character of Jesus Christ, the most perfect Man that ever lived, the only Savior of humanity, and my entire confidence in His teachings, as given in the New Testament."*

The United States Senate. *The United States, a Christian Nation.* Without dissent, March 3 1863, the United States Senate passed this resolution: *"Resolved, that devoutly recognizing the supreme Authority and just government of Almighty God in all the affairs of men and nations, and sincerely believing that no people, however great in numbers and resources, or however strong in the justness of their cause, can prosper without His favor, and at the same time, deploring the national offenses, which have provoked His righteous judgment, yet encouraged in this day of trouble by the assurance of His Word, to seek Him for succor, according to His appointed way, through Jesus Christ, the Senate of the United States do hereby request the President of the United States, by his proclamation, to designate and set apart a day for national prayer and humiliation."* Congressional Globe third session of the Thirty Seventh Congress, pages 1448 and 1501.

In accord with the above resolution, President Lincoln, March 30th, issued his proclamation. The following passages are quoted: *"Whereas, it is the duty of nations, as well as of men, to own their dependence upon the overruling power of God, to confess their sins and transgressions in humble sorrow, yet with assured hope that genuine repentance will lead to mercy and pardon, and to recognize the sublime truth announced by the Holy Scriptures, and proven by all history, that those nations only are blessed whose God is the Lord; and inasmuch as we know that, by His divine law, nations, like individuals, are subjected to punishments and chastisements in this world, may we not justly fear that the awful calamity of Civil War, which now desolates the land, may be but a punishment inflicted upon us for our presumptuous sins, to the needful end of our national reformation as a whole people… Intoxicated with unbroken success, we have become too self–sufficient to feel the necessity of redeeming and preserving grace, too proud to the God that made us."*

We need to remember and hold fast to the historic traditions and inspirational words of our founding fathers and our other great leaders. In July 1776, General George Washington ordered the appointment of a chaplain to each Army regiment, and in his 'General Orders' to his men was written

> *"The blessing and protection of Heaven are at all times necessary but especially so in times of public distress and danger— The General hopes and trusts that every officer and man will endeavour so to live, and act, as becomes a Christian Soldier, defending the dearest Rights and Liberties of his country."*

America is once again experiencing a time of public distress and potential danger. This danger threatens the very values and beliefs our great nation was founded upon. Whatever faith you practice, remember the greatness of the American experiment comes from our founder's commitment to freedom, based upon their understanding of God's providence. As Americans, we need to have grateful, humble and hopeful hearts and seek God's protection and blessings upon our nation, and its people.

My next book will contain all 352 American citations of religious faith and belief, as documented in Stephen Abbott Northrop's 1894 book A Cloud of Witnesses.

VI — The 9.12 Project and the Contract from America

Below are the 9 Principles and 12 Values as defined by Glenn Beck and used by the members of the non–partisan 9.12 Project. These principles and values are important, powerful, and worth your consideration. They go beyond concern for specific politics and instead encourage self–examination and improvement of personal character and qualities found in many of our founding fathers. Of course, we want these qualities in our leaders, but before we can make that demand, we need to instill these qualities into our own lives.

You will find many Americans who are both Tea Party and 9.12 Project members, but there are subtle differences between the two groups. It has been suggested that the Tea Party movement is driven by a desire to change specific aspects of our government, such as balancing the federal budget and eliminating the national debt. Whereas, the 9.12 Project is focused more on promoting personal qualities that cause its members to become more concerned about making government accountable, honest, ethical and transparent. In many cases, you'll find that both groups are concerned with similar issues. You can learn more at:

www.the912project.com

The 9 Principles

1. America Is Good.
2. God: I believe in God and He is the Center of my Life.
3. Honesty: I must always try to be a more honest person than I was yesterday.
4. Marriage and Family: The family is sacred.

5. Justice: If you break the law you pay the penalty.
6. Life, Liberty, and The Pursuit of Happiness: I have a right to life, liberty and pursuit of happiness, but there is no guarantee of equal results.
7. Charity: I work hard for what I have and I will share it with whom I want to.
8. On your right to disagree: It is not un–American for me to disagree with authority or to share my personal opinion.
9. Who works for whom?: The government works for me.

The 12 Values

Honesty, Reverence, Hope, Thrift, Humility, Charity, Sincerity, Moderation, Hard Work, Courage, Personal Responsibility, Gratitude

The Contract from America

contractfromamerica.com

The Contract from America is a document and website created by Tea Party Patriots, Inc. Over 450,000 online votes were cast in order to select America's most pressing problems, resulting in the top 10 agenda items listed below. Political leaders and concerned citizens have signed the online petition in support of these agenda items, to bring them to a national vote and to support individual rights and liberties, a limited government and economic freedom.

1. Protect the Constitution
2. Reject Cap and Trade
3. Demand a Balanced Budget

4. Enact Fundamental Tax Reform
5. Restore Fiscal Responsibility and Constitutionally Limited Government
6. End Runaway Government Spending
7. De–fund, Repeal, and Replace Government–run Health Care
8. Pass an 'All–of–the–Above' Energy Policy
9. Stop the Pork
10. Stop the Tax Hikes

VII – Paul Revere Rides Again

PRLP – The Paul Revere Liberty Project © ™

"Listen my children and you shall hear, Of the midnight ride of Paul Revere..." – Henry Wadsworth Longfellow

On the evening of April 18, 1775, Dr. Joseph Warren instructed Paul Revere to ride to Lexington, Massachusetts in order to warn Samuel Adams and John Hancock that British troops were marching to arrest them and to seize the patriot's supplies at Concord. To ensure that Adams and Hancock where warned, two other riders were also sent, William Dawes and Dr. Samuel Prescottm, each taking a different route.

When the British regulars arrived in Lexington on April 19, they were confronted for the first time by a tiny band of American patriots, our original 'Band of Brothers.' The first musket shot fired that day at the Battle at Lexington Green would forever be known as the 'Shot Heard Round the World,' and would mark the beginning of our War of Independence.

"Proclaim LIBERTY throughout all the Land unto all the Inhabitants thereof, Lev. XXV X" — the Bible verse cast into our original Liberty Bell

Over 235 years later, twenty–first century Paul Reveres will ride once more to alert our beleaguered nation. In each rider's hand will be a 'Liberty Bell,' and in his or her saddlebag, important parchments. As they ride through large cities, small towns and rural communities, with streets lined with anxious citizens, they will ring their Liberty Bell and loudly proclaim the good news that ***"Liberty is Coming! Liberty is Coming!"***

Let Freedom Ring

"This will be the day when all of God's children will be able to sing with a new meaning, 'My country, 'tis of thee, sweet land of liberty, of thee I sing. Land where my fathers died, land of the pilgrim's pride, from every mountainside, let freedom ring.'" – Martin Luther King Jr.

Starting on April 19, 2011 and each year thereafter, in communities throughout our nation, patriots will gather in front of their city halls while one or more horseback riders will travel throughout their community ringing their Liberty Bells and proclaiming *"Liberty is Coming! Liberty is Coming!"* The rider(s) will meet the patriots at their city hall at 6:00 PM, who will also be ringing their Liberty Bells and proclaiming *"Liberty is Coming! Liberty is Coming!"* They will then affix a copy of the 'Next Declaration of Independence' parchment to the front door of their city hall.

One year later, on April 19, 2012, Liberty will once again be proclaimed at city halls throughout the nation, but a special event will also take place that day to commemorate the 237th anniversary of Paul Revere's famous ride.

At midnight in Boston, a horseman (Paul Revere) will be rowed across the Charles River and will then ride through Charlestown, Medford, Menotomy, Lexington and on to Concord. A second horseback rider (William Dawes,) will ride west from Boston to Roxbury, Brookline, Cambridge, Menotomy, Lexington and on to Concord. A third horseback rider (Dr. Samuel Prescott) will ride from Lexington to Concord. Each rider will ring their Liberty Bell and proclaim *"Liberty is Coming! Liberty is Coming!"* to all those communities. From Concord, the riders and horses will then be transported to Arlington National Cemetery and the Tomb of the Unknown Soldier where a Liberty Wreath will be placed upon the tomb. After a prayer and a moment of silence, the three horseback riders will ride down Memorial Drive, across the Potomac River and ride on to the base of the Washington Monument.

Colonial war re–enactors playing the roles of George Washington, Thomas Jefferson, Benjamin Franklin, John Adams, Samuel Adams and others and colonial solders will meet the riders. The riders will present their parchments to our 'Founding Fathers' who will carry the parchments down the Mall, escorted by colonial solders, a colonial color–guard and a colonial marching band.

> *"What country can preserve its liberties if its rulers are not warned from time to time that their people preserve the spirit of resistance?" – Thomas Jefferson*

In front of the U.S. Capital will be two Colonial artillery batteries, one on the left side and one on the right side of a full–size replica of the Liberty Bell. As the founding fathers arrive, the Liberty Bell will be rung and the canons fired. Then our founders will ask the crowd to become quiet and a prayer of blessing will be offered for our nation.

A lone colonial solder will then march out onto the center of the Mall and fire his musket once into the air, signaling the 'Second Shot Heard Round the World,' and marking the beginning of our twenty–first century struggle to Reclaim Liberty. The founding fathers will then continue up the steps of the U.S. Capital building where they will affix 'The NEXT Declaration of Independence' parchment to the front door at 6:00 PM.

Across the country at 6:00 PM, the patriots who have gathered in front of their local city halls will ring their Liberty Bells for 1 minute and loudly proclaim the good news that *"Liberty is Coming! Liberty is Coming!"*

The riders will also be carrying parchments containing the printed names of the hundreds of thousands of American patriots who have signed their names online at:

www.ReclaimLiberty.us

These 'Parchments of Signators' and a second copy of 'The NEXT Declaration of Independence' will be presented to supportive members of congress on the steps of the U.S. Capital building, to be read aloud before both Houses of Congress.

In the 'The NEXT Declaration of Independence' will be written the following

The Next Declaration of the People of the United States of America

When in the course of American events, it becomes necessary for one people to examine and correct the government that unites them, and to assume their natural and God given rights to demand from their government honesty, transparency and respect for the collective will of the governed.

After over 234 years, We The People are once again compelled to proclaim that:

> *"We hold these truths to be self–evident, that all Americans are created equal, that they are endowed by their Creator with certain unalienable rights, that among these are Life, Liberty and the pursuit of Happiness."*

That to secure these rights, our representative form of government was established by and derives its power from the consent of the governed. As our government has become an obstruction to these purposes, it is the right and solemn duty of the governed to correct or abolish it, and to thus institute a reformed, or completely new government, laying its foundation on such principles, and organizing its powers in such a form as to effect the safety, happiness and will of the governed.

But after many years of unfulfilled promises, misconduct and abuse of power, it is the American people's right and solemn duty to repair, if possible, or throw off such government, and to establish new safeguards for our nation's security, prosperity and future. Such has been the patient, painful endurance of the American people, but now it becomes clear and necessary to alter our system of government. Many presidential and congressional histories are those of repeated injury to the very health of our nation, such as but not limited to:

- Not faithfully upholding their sworn 'Oaths' to preserve, protect, support, defend and bear true faith and allegiance to our Constitution
- Uncontrolled deficit spending, unsustainable foreign borrowing and unimaginable levels of National debt, all without mandates of the governed. These debts shake our nation to its very core and jeopardize its stability, security and future inheritance by our children
- Actively expanding the scope and size of the federal government while diminishing the authority of the states and the people, in direct opposition to the dire warnings of our Founding Fathers
- Costly mismanagement of public moneys, spent on bloated programs and failed policies
- Compromising our electoral processes for the sole purpose of restraining political challengers while retaining public office and power
- The dangerous and misguided belief that elected office should be a lifelong career, in direct opposition to the writings and examples set personally by our Founding Fathers
- Policies that overly intrude into individual rights and privacy
- Unchecked earmarks, special favors and pork–barrel spending, for the sole purpose of personal gain, power and reelection
- Unchallenged, unpunished and unethically corrupt behaviors including the negative influences of money and contributions and the compromising persuasions of lobbyists

- Continued passage of costly, unpopular, unfunded, unconstitutional legislations without the mandates of the governed
- Regulatory mismanagement of the economy, unfettered government bailouts and unjust, unneeded and unwanted intrusions into honest private businesses
- Overly complex and unfair taxation without true representation
- Policies that promote the redistribution of wealth from those that work to those that don't, in direct opposition to the written warnings of our Founding Fathers
- Programs that entrap and enslave citizens who become solely dependent upon government handouts and failed social program

In every stage of these oppressions, we have petitioned that our collective will would be heard and adhered to, and yet, our repeated wishes and objections have been answered only by continued injustice. In response, the American people declare a resounding 'No confidence' in the Federal Government. In addition to correcting or abolishing the above stated injuries, the American people demand that elected officials and Federal employees:

- Protect and uphold the Constitution; appoint nonpartisan Constitutional scholars to openly evaluate all federal legislations and procedures
- Pass a Constitutional amendment that enacts balanced federal budgets that do not exceed 20% of GDP; only allows federal borrowing after a 2/3 approval vote by the States; demands a rapid elimination of all federal debts and loans and requires that all current and future programs and mandates are either fully funded or eliminated

- Pass a Constitutional amendment that ensures that individual and States rights and laws supersede overreaching federal laws; that ensures that the federal government will demonstrate a strict respect and adherence to the collective will of the people; establishes a National Voter Initiative process for managing Congress and repealing bad laws
- Pass a Constitutional amendment that enacts Congressional Term Limits; places caps on congressional and federal employee salaries and benefits tied directly to the average American salary

We The People appeal to the Federal Government to adhere to our collective will, and in the name and by the authority of the American people, solemnly publish, declare and demand a limited, representative, accountable, ethical and transparent government. And for the support of this Declaration, with a firm reliance on the protection of Divine Providence and Rule of Law, we mutually pledge to each other our Lives, our Fortunes, and our Sacred Honor.

VIII – Who are WE THE PEOPLE?

An open letter to President Obama

Who are these Tea Party activists, Mr. President? As written in the U.S. Constitution, they are 'WE THE PEOPLE.' They are a grassroots movement of patriotic Americans who want a better government, a Constitutional republic, as envisioned by our founding fathers. The Independents, the Libertarians and the Republicans all understand this political movement.

You, the liberal congress and the left–wing media do not understand. Instead of embracing and encouraging this spontaneous, dynamic display of patriotic fervor and love for country, the left sees these patriots as a threat. The left has gone out of its way to ignore and marginalize them, question their loyalty, and even label them as racists.

You call yourself a 'racial uniter,' and yet in April 2010, you openly criticized and condemned the Governor and people of Virginia for not including references to slavery in their Confederacy Month Proclamation. And then you remained silent when your own party unjustly slandered Tea Party members with unfounded accusations of racism. Your acts and your omissions are not those of a uniter. And the passions of the Tea Party movement have nothing to do with race or the color of your skin, but instead, with the dark abyss of our government's soul.

The Tea Party patriots understand what's at stake. Long before you were even born, Mr. President, the progressive wheels of change were already turning. As our government drifted further away from our founder's Constitutional vision, the white–hot furnaces were already refining the iron that would be needed to forge our nation's financial shackles.

How can our free republic justify enslaving generations to come with unimaginable spending and debt? How can our government 'servants' condemn its nation to life–long debtor's servitude?

The Declaration of Independence states

"We hold these truths to be self–evident, that all men are created equal, that they are endowed by their Creator with certain unalienable Rights, that among these are Life, Liberty and the pursuit of Happiness."

WE THE PEOPLE have been Endowed with these Unalienable Rights by the Creator, and not by the government. How can we Pursue Happiness if our nation is harnessed to the crushing yoke of foreign debt? Even though we were Created Equal, is the serf truly equal to the landowner, or the debtor equal to the lender? Or has our government secretly revoked our Unalienable Rights of Equality?

The Declaration continues

"That to secure these rights, Governments are instituted among Men, deriving their just powers from the consent of the governed,"

Has our government exercised Just Powers in these matters? Have the Governed Consented to $1 trillion dollar deficits annually for the next 10 years? Have the Governed Consented to almost $122.5 trillion dollars of debt and unfunded mandates, and $1.1 billion in interest payments per day on our national debt?

The Declaration continues

"That whenever any Form of Government becomes destructive of these ends, it is the Right of the People to alter or to abolish it, and to institute new Government, laying its foundation on such principles and organizing its powers in such

form, as to them shall seem most likely to effect their Safety and Happiness"

Massive spending and foreign debt is Destructive to both the financial health and future of our nation. The People are neither Safe nor Happy while suffocating beneath this oppressive burden. Therefore, according to our sacred founding documents, WE THE PEOPLE have the right, and the duty, to alter or abolish any Destructive government, and institute a reformed or new government.

What will be the historic outcome, Mr. President? Will you and the congress change our government's course away from its fiscally destructive behavior? Or will WE THE PEOPLE be obligated, once again, to take it upon themselves to put an end to the many injustices that government has imposed upon us?

Is this the end of the Democratic Party?

Hot on the heals of Barack Obama's 2008 presidential victory, Democrats resoundingly proclaimed "The End of the Republican Party!" But history teaches us that your never turn your back on your opponent, because they may get back on their feet before the end of the 10–count.

Much has changed since the historic 1994 Republican Revolution. With "Contract with America" in hand, the late 20th century Republicans saw themselves as the rising Phoenix, the great conservative hope. They were energized, optimistic, and overconfident. The Contract included lofty promises, which pleased their constituents and sealed their impressive victory.

But as government grew and spending increased, the Republicans discarded Reagan's conservative compass. Even as the Contract grew dim and ethical scandals took their toll, the Republicans managed to maintain control of Congress through the remaining Clinton years and the first 6 years of Bush. But with growing public angst over the wars and the imploding economy, voters became mesmerized by a nebulous promise of a new political course, thus completing the overthrow of the Republican Revolution by a new regime.

And sixteen years after the Contract, its number–one promise is nowhere to be found: a balanced budget Constitutional amendment. Did the Republicans lose the political will to finally mandate fiscal responsibility, or did they begin to view their promise as a constraint to their own expanding aspirations? In hindsight, the current congressional Republicans probably lament the fact that they did not enact this overdue restraint.

Facing an unsettling future marked by Obama's trillion dollar annual deficits, 61 percent federal debt to GDP, $1.1 billion in national debt interest payments per day and $1.1 million owed by each U.S. taxpayer for federal debt and unfunded mandates, Fed Chairman Ben Bernanke, the Congressional Budget Office and a choir of respected economists all warn of a Greece–like train wreck if we don't put the nation's financial house in order. So it's now the Tea Party's turn to rekindled the hopes of 1994: fiscal responsibility, a balanced federal budget, and an end to "intergenerational larceny."

You may be asking: how do the Democrats fit into this retrospective? Just like the Republican Revolution, their current control of the White House and Congress has inflated Democratic arrogance. After 14–years on the sidelines, they now feel set–apart and anointed by the American voter, but this is a fickle voter. As the new–penny shine fads from their charismatic president, voter discontent has intensified over the ballooning debt, the monumentally unpopular healthcare legislation, and most importantly, the depressed economy and dismal jobs–front.

As the Democrats naively contemplate their next intransigent national conquests; immigration amnesty, the massive Cap–and–

Trade energy taxes and income redistribution; they move farther away from the voter's pressing concerns: employment, the economy and fiscal responsibility. And as the Democrats vilify the ever–growing Tea Party ranks of average American Joes and Josephines, while spending boatloads of borrowed foreign money in an insatiable orgy of union paybacks and social engineering, their brief honeymoon with America careens towards a tragic conclusion, if it hasn't already crashed and burned.

The question that Democratic strategists should be asking themselves is: how much damage are our boorish, obstinate policies causing, and how many years will it take for the voters to forgive and forget — once again?

To quote a cyclic trend: Is this the end of the Democratic Party? And after the November 2010 mid–term elections, will the Republicans be granted another 14–years in charge of the sandbox? Fourteen more years to, once again, fail to do "We the People's" fiscal bidding?

IX — Give Me Liberty, or Give Me Debt?

"The People have stirred from slumber. As Liberties diminish, loathing of government amplifies." – Robert J. Thorpe

There's an old saying *"You get the government you deserve."* For far too long, we have been silent and complacent, and thus have the government we deserve.

In his first primetime press conference on February 9, 2009, President Obama warned that a failure to pass his economic recovery plan (the Stimulus Plan) could *"turn a crisis into a catastrophe."* Obama stated *"But at this particular moment, with the private sector so weakened by this recession, the federal government is the only entity left with the resources to jolt our economy back into life. It is only government that can break the vicious cycle where lost jobs lead to people spending less money which leads to even more layoffs."*

Exactly which resources was the President referring to? Can borrowing even more money from the Chinese government, and placing our nation further into debt, really be considered a resource?

"Were we directed from Washington when to sow and when to reap, we should soon want bread" — Thomas Jefferson

According to the April 3, 2010 New York Times story, *Start–Ups, Not Bailouts,* Thomas L. Friedman stated that

"Between 1980 and 2005, virtually all net new jobs created in the U.S. were created by firms that were 5 years old or less. That is about 40 million jobs."

In the April 26, 2010 Real Clear Politic story, *Hold the VAT — Taxpayers May Prefer Spending Cuts,* Michael Barone writes that about one–third of the $862 billion February 2009 stimulus

package went to state and local governments in order to prevent 'interruption of services.' But while the private sector lost almost 8 million jobs, the public sector lost almost no jobs. Barone sees this as 'payback' for the public employee labor unions, which had heavily contributed to Obama and the Democrats during the 2008 elections.

Although our nation has a history of small private sector businesses leading the way out of recession and fueling economic growth, the $862 billion Stimulus Plan provided few resources for small businesses. It instead focused on protecting state and local government 'union' jobs and government programs such as roads, research grants and 'underpasses for turtles.' During this same period, Obama also predicted that without the Stimulus Plan, unemployment would hit 8 percent.

According to Stephen Gandel's Times story, unemployment hit 9.5 percent by July 2009, the highest level it had reached in 26 years. In actuality, 'with' the Stimulus Plan, we've seen unemployment go beyond 10 percent nationally, and in some regions, surpass 14 percent.

Government doesn't create the jobs that create wealth and prosperity in our country, the private sector does. Large government bureaucracies increase the burdens on taxpayers and businesses and stifle private sector growth. According to Thomas Jefferson's quote below, government should leave people (and their businesses) alone, free to regulate their own pursuits. Government can help the private sector when it facilitates job creation and growth by promoting a well–educated workforce and free foreign trading markets, all with few if any government restraints and regulations. If nothing else, it can be most helpful by simply getting out of our way.

"A wise and frugal government, which shall restrain men from injuring one another, which shall leave them otherwise

free to regulate their own pursuits of industry and improvement, and shall not take from the mouth of labor and bread it has earned. This is the sum of good government" — Thomas Jefferson

Our founding fathers envisioned a limited federal government where the states and the people were protected from government abuse. Instead, we have a government that grows larger and more powerful with every new administration.

Liberty is Decreasing

"The proposition that the people are the best keepers of their own liberties is not true. They are the worst conceivable, they are no keepers at all; they can neither judge, act, think, or will, as a political body" — John Adams

In the April 2010 American Spectator story, *Out of Control,* Dick Armey writes

"Our Founding Fathers designed a Constitutional system based on the rule of law to protect the individual from an overbearing federal government. The government was to do only that which was both right and necessary; the rest was to be left up to the States and individuals."

The founding fathers hoped that the Constitution would keep a power–hungry central government limited in size and constrained. But what we have now is a federal government that often ignores its citizens and the rules and limits as defined in the Constitution.

At the October 29, 2009 press conference, a CNSNews.com reporter asked House Speaker Nancy Pelosi: *"Madam Speaker, where specifically does the Constitution grant Congress the authority to enact an individual health insurance mandate?"* Speaker Pelosi responded, *"Are you serious? Are you serious?"* The reporter said, *"Yes, yes, I am."* Not responding further, Pelosi shook her head and took a question from another reporter.

Speaker Pelosi and many of her colleagues have simply chosen to ignore the 10th Amendment to the Bill of Rights, which states

> *"The powers not delegated to the United States by the Constitution, nor prohibited by it to the States, are reserved to the States respectively, or to the people"*

For congress to pass a law, whether large (like ObamaCare) or small, their authority either needs to have already been granted to them by the Constitution, or the States, by a 3/4 vote, would need to ratify a new Constitutional amendment granting congress the specific, required authority. If neither is the case, then congress does not have the authority, and the states or the people would need to pass the law themselves.

> *"The two enemies of the people are criminals and government, so let us tie the second down with the chains of the Constitution so the second will not become the legalized version of the first" — Thomas Jefferson*

The writings of our founding fathers show a solemn reverence for, and faith in our Constitution. Their hope was that they had successfully laid the framework to hold back tyranny from infecting their new government. The tyranny they tried to prevent in our country was the same type of tyranny that America had just successfully fought King George III and the British Empire, in order to win our independence.

> *"An elective despotism was not the government we fought for" — Thomas Jefferson*

In the April 4, 2010 Washington Post story, *The Poisonous Politics of Self–Esteem,* Robert Samuelson writes

Purging moral questions from politics is both impossible and undesirable. But today's tendency to turn every contentious issue into a moral confrontation is divisive. It's easier to portray the 'other side' as scum: the more scummy 'they' are, the more superior 'we' are.

Dangers are plain, as political scientists Morris Fiorina and Samuel Abrams argue in their book *Disconnect: the Breakdown of Representation in American Politics.* They show that polarization is stronger among elites (elected officials, activists, journalists) than the broad public.

About 40 – 50 percent of Americans classify themselves as 'moderates,' whereas political activists tend to identify themselves as 'very liberal' or 'very conservative.' But it is the political class of activists that 'dominate the political agenda' and determine 'how the debate is conducted.' The ultimate danger is that the poisonous polarization of elites spreads to the country at large.

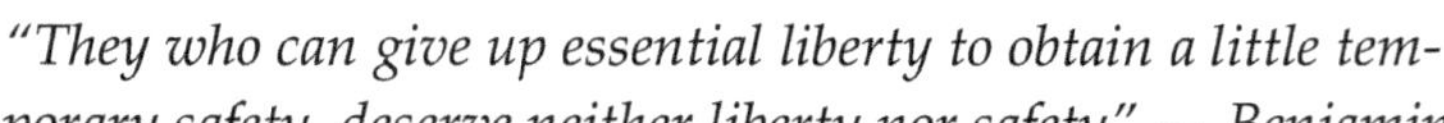

"They who can give up essential liberty to obtain a little temporary safety, deserve neither liberty nor safety" — Benjamin Franklin

We have tyranny when our elected officials and public servants demonstrate elitist attitudes, dismiss the will of the people and treat the public with contempt. After hundreds of peaceful Tea Party rallies and spirited congressional town hall meetings over healthcare reform and government fiscal policies, in February 2010 on ABC news, Democratic House Speaker Nancy Pelosi smeared the Tea Party movement as *"directed by the GOP"* and *"Astroturf, as opposed to grassroots."*

The very passage of ObamaCare demonstrated government's contempt for the will of the people. For almost a year, there were marches, rallies, town hall meetings and months of polling that showed that the nation was opposed to the legislation by a margin of 2 to 1. Flouting congressional history and tradition of always needing a super–majority for the passage of major new legislation, congress instead violated the will of the people and rammed the healthcare law through using unimaginable parliamentary tricks, never before used with such a monumental, far–reaching bill. And the only bipartisan votes were those opposed to the bill.

This brings to mind a quote from Princess Amidala in the movie Star Wars, Episode III – Revenge of the Sith *"So this is how liberty dies... with thunderous applause."*

The Food Police and a Not so 'Happy Meal'

In the April 27, 2010 Los Angeles Times story, *Happy Meal toys could be banned in Santa Clara County,* Sharon Bernstein writes

> A county supervisor has created a stir with his proposal to bar the inclusion of toys (not food) in restaurant meals that contain high amounts of sugar, salt or certain fats. Convinced that Happy Meals could make kids fat as well as happy, county officials in Silicon Valley are poised to outlaw the little toys that often come with high–calorie offerings.
>
> The proposed ban is the latest in a growing string of efforts to change the types of foods aimed at youngsters and the way they are cooked and sold. Across the nation, cities, states and school boards have taken aim at excessive sugar, salt and certain types of fats.
>
> Believed to be the first of its kind in the nation, the proposal would forbid the inclusion of a toy in any res-

> taurant meal that has more than 485 calories, more than 600 mg of salt or high amounts of sugar or fat. In the case of McDonald's, the limits would include all of the chain's Happy Meals — even those that include apple sticks instead of French fries.
>
> Supporters say the ban would encourage restaurants to offer more–nutritious foods to kids and would make unhealthful items less appealing. But opponents believe it amounts to government meddling in parental decisions.

It seems like such a small thing, but taking away a child's toy in order to modify social behavior is another example of government intrusion on both businesses and on the lives of individuals. The political elite believes that they always know what's best, but in this case, their mandates would amount to a nanny–state and the decline of parent and children's personal liberties and freedom of choice.

No one would argue against children, and even their parents, eating healthier foods and getting more exercise. And the cheap plastic toy, destined for a landfill, probably shouldn't be made from our dwindling oil reserves. However, is this the best way for government (or the Food Police), with no specific mandate in this area from the governed, to deal with what they deem a social problem? Instead of enacting heavy–handed laws for taking toys (or candy) away from babies, government could provide free education to teach parents about exercise and nutrition. Parents, children and society might all benefit while retaining free choice and personal liberty.

The Politics of Race

In the July 06, 2010 FoxNews.com story, *Ex–Official Accuses Justice Department of Racial Bias in Black Panther Case*

> Ex–Justice official J. Christian Adams, who quit over the handling of a voter intimidation case against the New Black Panther Party, accused the Justice Department of instructing attorneys in the civil rights division to ignore cases involving black defendants and white victims.
>
> Testifying Tuesday before the U.S. Commission on Civil Rights, Adams said that *"over and over and over again,"* the department showed *"hostility"* toward those cases. The Panther's case was one example— Adams defended the legitimacy of the suit and said his *"blood boiled"* when a Justice official claimed the case wasn't solid.
>
> *"We abetted wrongdoing and abandoned law–abiding citizens,"* Adams later testified.
>
> Last year, Justice abandoned the case that stemmed from a 2008 Philadelphia Election Day incident where members of the Panthers were videotaped in front of a polling place, dressed in military–style uniforms, and allegedly hurled racial slurs while one brandished a night stick.
>
> But as the investigation unfolded, Adams said he discovered *"indications"* that the Panthers had done the *"same thing"* to supporters of former presidential candidate Hillary Clinton during early 2008 Democratic primaries. Adams urged the commission to pursue testimony from other Justice officials to corroborate his story.

In the April 6, 2010 Real Clear Politics story, *Race and Politics,* Thomas Sowell writes that 'race and politics' can be attributed to the slaughter of millions, and has torn nations apart.

> You might think we would have learned a lesson and stay away from injecting race into political issues. Yet playing the race card has become an increasingly common response to growing public anger at the policies of the Obama administration and the way those policies have been imposed.
>
> When the triumphant Democrats made their widely televised walk up Capitol Hill after passing the healthcare bill, led by a smirking and strutting Nancy Pelosi holding her oversized gavel, some of the crowd of citizens expressed their anger. According to some Democrats, these expressions of anger included racial slurs directed at black members of congress.
>
> This is a serious charge— and one deserving of some serious evidence. But despite all the media recording devices on the scene, not to mention recording devices among the crowd gathered there, nobody can come up with a single recorded sound to back up that incendiary charge. Worse yet, some people have claimed that even doubting the charge suggests that you are a racist.

"America will never be destroyed from the outside. If we falter and lose our freedoms, it will be because we destroyed ourselves" — Abraham Lincoln

In the November 5, 2008 Politico story, *Exit polls: How Obama Won,* David Paul Kuhn wrote

> Barack Obama, who will be the nation's first African–American president, won the largest share of white sup-

port of any Democrat in a two–man race since 1976 amid a backdrop of economic anxiety unseen in at least a quarter–century, according to exit polls by The Associated Press and the major television networks.

Many of the same people who supported and voted for President Obama in 2008, but have now become disenchanted and dissatisfied with his leadership, are now branded as racists. Surprisingly, the racist charges have not only been limited to white people, but are also hurled at blacks as well.

As reported in the April 06, 2010 Associated Press story, *Black Tea Party Activists Called Traitors*

> *"I've been told I hate myself. I've been called an Uncle Tom. I've been told I'm a spook at the door,"* said Timothy F. Johnson, chairman of the Frederick Douglass Foundation, a group of black conservatives who support free market principles and limited government.
>
> *"I've gotten the statement, 'How can you not support the brother?'"* said David Webb, an organizer of New York City's Tea Party 365, Inc. movement and a conservative radio personality. Since Obama's election, Webb said some black conservatives have even resorted to hiding their political views. *"I know of people who would play the (liberal) role publicly, but have their private opinions,"* he said. *"They don't agree with the policy but they have to work, live and exist in the community ... Why can't we speak openly and honestly if we disagree?"*
>
> Angela McGlowan, a black congressional candidate from Mississippi, said her tea party involvement is *"not about a black or white issue. It's not even about Republican or Democrat, from my standpoint,"* she told The Associated

Press. *"All of us are taxed too much."* Some black conservatives credit President Barack Obama's election, and their distaste for his policies, with inspiring them and motivating dozens of black Republicans to plan political runs in November. *"I'm so proud to be a part of this (Tea Party) movement. I want to tell you that a lot of people underestimate you guys,"* the former national political commentator for Fox News told the cheering crowd at a Tea Party rally in Nashville, Tenn., in February.

In an Associated Press April 09, 2010 story, *Obama Criticizes Virginia Governor (Bob McDonnell) for Slavery Omission in Confederacy Month Proclamation*

"I don't think you can understand the Confederacy and the Civil War unless you understand slavery," said Obama. On Wednesday, McDonnell apologized and added a paragraph condemning slavery, saying that leaving it out had been a *"major omission."* Obama said the controversy was *"a reminder that when we talk about issues like slavery that are so fraught with pain and emotion, that, you know, we'd better do so thinking through how this is going to affect a lot of people."*

In a FoxNews.com April 11, 2010 story, *Mississippi Gov. Barbour Backs McDonnell on 'Confederate History' Declaration*

Mississippi Gov. Haley Barbour on Sunday defended fellow Gov. Bob McDonnell for his decision to declare April 'Confederate History Month' in Virginia without initially acknowledging the legacy of slavery, saying the controversy *"doesn't amount to diddly."*

"I don't know what you would say about slavery, but anybody that thinks that you have to explain to people that slavery is a bad thing, I think that goes without saying," he told CNN's 'State of the Union.'

What's troubling about Obama's statements is that McDonnell didn't bring up the divisive issue of slavery in the first place, the President did. Was this truly a 'controversy,' and should the good people of the South be branded forever for the mistakes of the past? It appears that some in our nation would continuously remind, and even require us to keep opening–up old wounds simply for the sake of 'Political Correctness.' Perhaps instead, we should be striving to heal those wounds while building a better nation, a nation with liberty and justice for all.

There are many people in our nation, especially within the black community, who have been oppressed by their liberal leaders for generations. Legacies of failed social programs where politicians have only given lip service, and little else, to the plights of the inner–cities and rural communities, which continue to languish under failed government policies. Unfortunately, these cycles cannot be broken until the people force their government to change course. But this can only take place when it begins in the homes, families and neighbors who have unknowingly perpetuated the lie that liberal politicians are looking out for the people's best interest.

We are living in troubling times.

"I have sworn on the altar of God eternal hostility against every form of tyranny over the mind of man" — Thomas Jefferson

ObamaCare

"That government is best which governs least" – Henry David Thoreau

The new healthcare law could encompass a volume of books by itself. Here are a few points about this tyrannical new law and how for the first time in our nation's history, congress has used the unprecedented, unconstitutional use of the 'Commerce Clause' to force private citizens to purchase a product, in this case, health insurance.

In his April 9, 2010 National Review op–ed piece, *Unconstitutional Mandate,* Virginia Attorney General Kenneth T. Cuccinelli II wrote about why the Virginia governor and legislature had passed a bipartisan anti–mandate law, the 'Health Care Freedom Act,' in order to block ObamaCare's mandate to force Virginia citizens to purchase health insurance.

Cuccinelli states that the federal government has never used the Commerce Clause of the Constitution to force citizens to purchase goods or services. Article I, Section 8 of the Constitution provides that *"the Congress shall have Power... To regulate Commerce with Foreign Nations, and among the several States."*

An individual mandate to purchase health insurance is not intrastate commerce, where *"the use of law to impose reason and order on the voluntary commercial actions of citizens, as well as on activities that substantially affect commerce."*

According to Cuccinelli, the healthcare law is also an off the books income redistribution / funding mechanism. The law forces young and healthy people to purchase overpriced insurance for the purpose of subsidizing the old and those with pre–existing conditions. One of the drafters, Senator Max Baucus, chairman of the Senate Finance Committee, admitted during the Senate reconciliation debate, *"This is also an income shift. This legislation will have the effect of addressing... mal–distribution of income in America."*

The Sixteenth Amendment authorizes the progressive income tax, which is the traditional source of the federal government's authority to create social Welfare programs. The use of a purchasing mandate instead crosses an important Constitutional line. Congress does not have the power to force Americans to buy overpriced products from private companies for the purpose of income redistribution.

In response, Virginia's governor and legislature adopted the new anti–mandate law, the Health Care Freedom Act. The law, which is in direct conflict with the federal healthcare bill, states that in Virginia, citizens cannot be compelled to purchase health insurance against their will. Virginia's challenge to the healthcare bill is not just about buying insurance, but it's also about limiting the power of the federal government over Virginia citizens, and protecting their liberties.

In the April 12, 2010 Real Clear Politics story, *ObamaCare and the Supreme Court,* Michael Barone writes about the possibility of a Supreme Court candidate being asked about the Constitutionality of the new healthcare law. Tough Constitutional questions of any Supreme Court candidate, concerning the unpopular healthcare law, would probably help the Republican party in the November 2010 mid–term elections.

Fourteen state's attorneys generals are currently suing the federal government over the healthcare law, arguing that the Commerce Clause of the Constitution does not allow the government to force citizens to purchase a product.

Another argument concerns a citizen's right to privacy. A pivotal principle in the cases of Griswold vs. Connecticut and Roe vs. Wade, is whether privacy is protected under the new law, where government now has an active, intrusive role in healthcare. According to former New York Lt. Gov. Betsy McCaughey, *"Either your body is protected from government interference, or it's not."*

Barone goes on to quote McCaughey about the 2006 Gonzales v. Oregon case. The Supreme Court ruled that Oregon's 'Death with Dignity' act was immune from government regulation of doctors administering lethal drugs to terminally ill patients. But if government cannot regulate 'lethal drugs' in Oregon, how can it regulate non–lethal drugs in the rest of the country?

Many Americans would complain loudly about losing their liberties if (when) politicians took away their freedom to choose what they eat by forcing them to only eat food that the government thinks is best. This is what happens in a nanny–state, where 'government knows best.'

Now that our government is in the healthcare business, they are suddenly concerned about keeping us well. But this sudden interest in our well–being probably has more to do with keeping government medical costs low, than it does with our quality of life. Welcome to the 'Food Police State,' a rather unsavory state indeed.

In the April 20, 2010 Reuters story, *FDA should regulate salt, panel says,* Julie Steenhuysen writes

> U.S. regulators are planning a push to gradually cut the amount of salt Americans consume, saying less sodium would reduce deaths from hypertension and heart disease. The effort would eventually lead to the first legal limits on the amount of salt allowed in processed foods.

The government plans to work with the food industry and health experts to reduce sodium gradually over a period of years, to ratchet down sodium consumption.

U.S. researchers said in a recent study that, working with the food industry to cut salt intake by nearly 10 percent, could prevent hundreds of thousands of heart attacks and strokes over several decades and save the U.S. government $32 billion in healthcare costs. Eating too much salt is a major cause of high blood pressure, which the Institute of Medicine last week declared a 'neglected disease' that costs the U.S. health system $73 billion a year.

To quote Vice President Biden, ObamaCare is a ***"Big F–ing Deal,"*** and between now and the November 2010 midterm elections, it will probably get bigger. Perhaps ObamaCare, and our coming 'Food Police State,' will be a rallying cry for finally mobilizing our citizenry to fight for their nation's liberties and economic survival.

For your November 2010 voting reference (and reading enjoyment), the last chapter of this handbook lists all of 219 House Representatives who voted 'Aye' or Yes for ObamaCare, H.R. 3590, on March 21, 2010.

"What country can preserve its liberties if its rulers are not warned from time to time that their people preserve the spirit of resistance?" — Thomas Jefferson

Divide and Conquer

In the April 9, 2010 National Review story, *Our American Catharsis,* Victor Davis Hanson writes about how much has changed in the past year, especially people's attitudes.

In just a year, the manner in which Americans look at things has changed radically. Something as mundane as buying a Ford or a GM car now takes on ideological connotations: The former company, in politically recalcitrant fashion, resists government takeover; the latter has been transmogrified from Michael Moore's Roger & Me bogeyman into a sanctioned, government–subsidized brand. Toyota went from the good green maker of the Prius to a foreign corporate outlaw whose handful of faulty accelerators symbolizes the non–union threat to fair–play American production.

The whole notion of capital and debt has changed, mostly on the issue of culpability. Buying too much house at too high interest is the bank's fault. Not being able to pay a debt is certainly negotiable and most certainly nothing to feel bad about. Maxing out credit cards and getting caught with high interest is proof of corporate malfeasance. Cash in the bank earns little, if any, interest. Owing lots of money costs little, and it does not necessarily have to be paid back, if one is able to stake a persuasive claim against 'them.'

The reaction to a hated and greedy Wall Street is now to be an omnipotent, all–wise, and all–caring state technocracy. Today there is nothing so simplistic as the actual 'unemployment rate'; 'jobs saved' by government borrowing is the better barometer of who is actually working and who is not. A $200–billion shortfall is a 'deficit'; a trillion dollar one is 'stimulus.'

Not purchasing a cheap catastrophic healthcare plan is quite understandable. The Department of Motor Vehicles, Amtrak, and the Postal Service are models of what good government can do. Social Security and Medicare

are not unsustainable or insolvent; those loaded adjectives are simply constructs of a wealthy class unwilling to pay the taxes needed to fund them.

Worrying about the deficit or national debt is a neurotic tic. Why fret, when millions in the oppressing class have enough money to eliminate these problems whenever we acquire the backbone to make them pay what they owe us? We are in a them / us, winners / losers zero–sum age, one in which a forever static pie must have its finite slices radically reapportioned.

When government openly vilifies oil companies, GM executives, bankers, Wall Street, health insurance and credit card companies, it creates an 'Us vs. Them' mentality that allows individuals to justify their irresponsible behaviors, like not paying their personal debts. This also empowers an entitlement mentality. If my credit card bills are too high, or I can't afford the high mortgage payments on my expensive home, or if I choose to buy an HD TV instead of health insurance, it's someone else's fault, not mine.

Our government simply reassures us that 'It's not your fault' and then 'forgives' our debts in a somewhat Christ–like manner through expensive government bailouts. However, it is important to consider who eventually pays, because in the end, someone always does. We all pay, either through higher taxes (pay now), or through the moneys that the government borrows from the Chinese (pay much more latter), or through higher fees charged by those 'evil' corporations that the government has just enabled us to morally and legally abuse.

At the very basic level, we need food, clean water, clothing and shelter to survive. Personal responsibility means that we live modestly and purchase those things we truly need and can afford. Do we really need an over–priced luxury home that we can't afford, or are we entitled to an $800 Apple iPad because it's the latest and greatest gadget? Simply charging those things we want, and really don't need, leads to twenty–four percent interest rates on $15,000 credit card balances. And when we find ourselves drowning in a sea of debt, we either file for bankruptcy protection or call on the government to bail us out. This is simply greedy, unsustainably, irresponsibly behavior. We have no one to blame but ourselves.

Death and Taxes

> *"I think myself that we have more machinery of government than is necessary, too many parasites living on the labor of the industrious" — Thomas Jefferson*

At what point do taxes become tyrannical? The following are highlights of Jonah Goldberg's April6, 2010 USA Today opinion piece.

> The Tax Foundation calculates that this year's Tax Freedom Day is April 9, 2010. Americans will have spent nearly 100 days working just to pay their taxes. And if government has its way, Tax Freedom Day will keep getting later and later in the year.
>
> If Tax Freedom Day became December 31, you'd be working 365 days a year for the government. The government could then 'give' you a place to sleep, food to eat and clothes to wear, and all your income would actually be Washington's income, to use and allocate as it sees fit.
>
> Some might call this sort of arrangement 'socialism' or 'communism.' But other perfectly good words for it are slavery, involuntary servitude or a nanny–state. Any

amount of taxation can be unjust if it's being used for bad reasons, is applied discriminatorily or if it's taken without representation.

When the government levies tax obligations on generations yet to come, our grandchildren are saddled with the debt of others, even though they did not have any representation in the taxation. The Tax Foundation estimates that some 60 percent of American families get more from the government than they pay in taxes, and that the top 10 percent of income earners pay more than 70 percent of the U.S. income taxes.

To make matters worse, Senate Finance Committee Chairman Max Baucus, (D–MT), recently admitted that alleviating the *"mal–distribution of income in America"* from the haves to the have–nots is one of ObamaCare's real benefits. But no matter how dumb America's wealth–creators might be, they're smart enough to respond to government incentives and disincentives appropriately. Since 1950, no matter where tax rates have been, from 28 percent to 91 percent, the government's 'take' has held steady at about 19.5 percent of GDP. This suggests that squeezing taxpayers harder doesn't actually yield more revenues. Our income tax system, which is made idiotically complex by both parties, demands countless hours of preparation and requires law abiding citizens to reveal many of their most private decisions to government inspectors every year.

"And so, my fellow Americans: ask not what your country can do for you – ask what you can do for your country. My fellow citizens of the world: ask not what America will do for

you, but what together we can do for the freedom of man" — John F. Kennedy

The April 07, 2010 New York Post story describes the government' s latest new tax idea, the European VAT.

> Obama Economic Adviser Says U.S. Should Consider Value Added Tax (or a national sales tax), acknowledging it would be a highly unpopular move. White House economic adviser Paul Volcker said yesterday the United States should consider imposing a 'value added tax' similar to those charged in Europe to help get the deficit under control. Volcker, at the New York Historical Society, told a panel on the global financial crisis that Congress might also have to consider new taxes on carbon and energy. The VAT suggestion was immediately met with outrage by Republicans. *"It shouldn't surprise anyone that the Obama White House would advocate a European–style tax to help finance their European–style government health–care plan,"* said Brian Walsh, a spokesman for the National Republican Senatorial Campaign Committee.

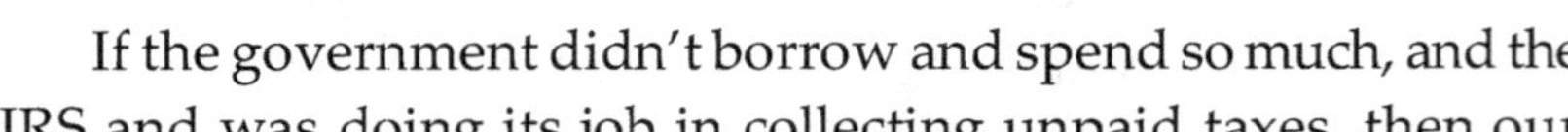

If the government didn't borrow and spend so much, and the IRS and was doing its job in collecting unpaid taxes, then our taxes wouldn't have to keep dramatically increasing.

In the April 20, 2010 FoxNews.com story, *IRS Targets Taxpayers Hiding Income in Offshore Accounts,* Jim Angle writes that the IRS is not aggressively finding American's taxable income hidden in offshore accounts.

> An estimated 19,000 American citizens were hiding taxable assets in the Swiss Bank UBS with the encouragement and assistance of the bank itself, the government alleges. UBS is now cooperating and has paid a

$780 million fine to avoid prosecution. *"It's amazing that the IRS had not actually come across this before,"* said Ken Kies, former chief of staff of the Congressional Joint Committee on Taxation.

Tom Ochsenschlager, President of Taxation for the American Institute of Certified Public Accountants, noted that the federal government has a tax gap of $300 billion a year. 'That's the difference between what should have been paid and what was not paid through the U.S. tax system.'

This begs the question: is the power to tax infinite? Is expecting or demanding our government to reduce its massive borrowing and spending unreasonable or unthinkable?

Spending into Oblivion

"Facts are stubborn things; and what ever may be our wishes, our inclinations, or the dictates of our passions, they cannot alter the state of facts, and evidence" — John Adams

As our nation's debts increase, our liberties decrease.

On January 8, 2009, President–Elect Obama said *"Government at every level will have to tighten its belt."* And yet we've seen massive increases in the size and cost of government since that speech.

According to the March 18, 2010 National Review story, *House GOP: Obamacare's IRS Connection,* Robert Costa writes that the healthcare law is adding $10 billion dollars of new public spending and bureaucracy to the IRS.

The House GOP's analysis of CBO scores indicate that ObamaCare will dole out as much as $1 billion per year to the IRS. Based on the current costs to employ this division's workforce, an additional $1 billion per year would mean 12,500 new IRS employees (agents) examining taxpayer records and fining those citizens without health insurance coverage. The IRS will impose the government's requirement that everyone has 'affordable' and 'acceptable' insurance coverage. In fact, they will be helping to achieve ObamaCare's eventual goal of forcing people into government–run insurance.

There are many serious concerns facing our nation today, but the most egregious are the federal government's out of control borrowing, debt and spending. According to a March 29, 2010 Chicago Tribune Editorial, the nonpartisan Congressional Budget Office offers this prognosis of future debt.

"Under the President's budget, debt held by the public would grow from $7.5 trillion (53 percent of GDP) at the end of 2009 to $20.3 trillion (90 percent of GDP) at the end of 2020."

When this happens, interest payments, which are currently at about $400 billion per year, would quadruple to about $1.6 trillion per year, which is $4.4 billion per day or $183 million per hour.

How can the federal government spend so much money? Here's some small examples from the Bureau of Labor Statistics. The federal government pays its employees considerably more than similar positions in the private sector. For example, a federal cook makes $15,121 more, a federal graphic designer makes $24,255 more and a federal public relations manager makes $44,169 more per year than similar positions in the private sector.

The federal government made history in February 2010. After only receiving $107 billion in tax revenue, they spent over $328 billion in just one month. Remember how shocking it was 10 – 15 years ago when the federal budget exceeded $1 trillion for the whole year. Now they've spent 1/3 of a trillion dollars in just 28 days. This unimaginable sum breaks down to $11.7 billion per day or $488.2 million per hour. Then add our $1.1 billion per day interest payments on the national debt, and our government spent $529.9 million (or over one half of a billion) dollars per hour in February. In contrast, the annual 'yearly' deficits under Bush's Republican controlled congress have now become the 'monthly' deficits under the Obama Democrats. For example, the Republican congress deficit for 2006 was $161 billion. Four years later, the 2010 Obama deficit is projected at $1.6 trillion, a 1,000 percent or 10 fold increase over the Republicans.

In the April 28, 2010 Washington Examiner story, *Media still clueless about Tea Parties,* Noemie Emery writes

> Obama began with a $787 billion stimulus package (which most economists have now dismissed as a failure), passed a fiscal 2010 budget of $3.5 trillion, passed a fiscal 2011 budget of $3.8 trillion, and passed his health care reform bill, for additional trillions whose scope we don't know. The 2010 spending is estimated at $9 trillion.

"All the perplexities, confusion and distress in America arise, not from defects in their Constitution or Confederation, not from want of honor or virtue, so much as from the downright ignorance of the nature of coin, credit and circulation" — John Adams

The federal government is currently spending more than double the amount of money it collects in taxes. Each taxpayer personally owes over $118,700 of our $13.1 trillion national debt. Unfunded entitlements (Social Security, Medicare, Prescription Drug, Welfare) is over $109.2 trillion, or $989,400 per taxpayer. Added together, each taxpayer owes almost $1.1 million in federal commitments. Our nation's interest payment on the national debt alone is currently about $400 billion per year or more than $1.1 billion per day. Please visit the www.USdebtclock.org to view the most current U.S. debt projections.

In his 2010book, *To Save America,* Newt Gingrich suggests

> That President Obama is building a secular socialist machine that will increase government dependency through new entitlements. With a 1/3 increase in Welfare spending in Obama's first two years alone, total government Welfare spending is now projected to be $10.3 trillion over the next 10 years.

Michael Barone's March 25, 2010 Real Clear Politics story describes how our nation's AAA bond rating may soon be down–graded, which would drastically increase our nation's costs when borrowing money.

Barone quotes former CBO Director, Douglas Holtz–Eakin New York Time's story that the CBO cost estimates of the healthcare law did not include

- $70 billion for long–term care premiums
- $114 billion in discretionary spending needed to run the program

- And includes nearly $500 billion dollars in unrealistic Medicare savings

The healthcare law will raise the deficit by $562 billion over 10 years, money the Treasury Department will have to borrow. Anticipated tax increases will retard economic growth and reduce government revenues, causing even more borrowing and possibly lowering the U.S. bond rating, which would cause the nation's debt interest rates to increase even more.

Holtz–Eakin predicts *"train wrecks ahead — as the bond market forces huge spending cuts or tax increases first on states and then on the federal government."*

In the April 5, 2010 San Francisco Chronicle story, *National debt seen heading for crisis level,* Carolyn Lochhead quoted the March 2010 CBO report that Obama's budget will add $10 trillion to the national debt in the next decade. There will be $5.6 trillion in interest costs alone in the next 10 years with a 63 percent Debt–to–GDP ratio this year and a 90 percent Debt–to–GDP ratio anticipated within this decade.

What is the solution to our huge, looming economic catastrophe? We should bail out the E.U. country of Greece, of course. However, when you consider that the U.S. is the largest contributor to the International Monetary Fund (IMF), and that our national debt to GDP will be approaching that of Greece in just a matter of a few years, the question then becomes 'who is going to bail us out?'

In the May 8, 2010New York Post story, *We're bailing out Greece, But U.S. taxpayers shouldn't be,* Mike Pence and Cathy McMorris Rodgers write

> As the largest contributor to the IMF, U.S. taxpayers will be helping to foot the bill for the Greek bailout and

may soon be on the line for even more and larger European 'rescues.'

Our unemployment rate stands at nearly 10 percent. The public debt now stands at $9.2 trillion. The Congressional Budget Office predicts that America's debt will reach 90 percent of gross domestic product within 10 years under President Obama's budget. Without dramatic spending restraints, America is on a path like the one that led to Greece's financial catastrophe.

In fact, Federal Reserve Chairman Ben Bernanke recently warned congress that without significant spending restraints, the United States would soon face a debt crisis like the one in Greece.

It is unfair and unwise to ask U.S. taxpayers to fund bailouts for EU countries while America racks up huge deficits of its own.

"The course of history shows that as government grows, liberty decreases" — Thomas Jefferson

As a nation, we cannot survive these levels of debt, spending and foreign borrowing. Did your federal representatives ever ask you specifically for permission to spend these unimaginable sums, and to saddle each taxpayer, and those to come, with $1.1 million or more of debt? No, and yet, why were we silent? Why didn't we protest years ago?

The federal government has proven itself to be an out of control, unrepentant, money junkie. It will never rehabilitate itself willingly. It's up to the people to stop the federal government's insatiable hunger to spend money.

Please note: The Obama administration's fiscal policies have been cited and highlighted numerous times in this handbook because they are relevant to our nation's current economic problems, and are of great concern to many Americans. Some may rightly argue that our current borrowing and spending is the worst that our nation has ever seen, but other recent administrations have also acted fiscally irresponsible, including George W. Bush.

In the February 24, 2009 Washington Examiner story, *Obama's trillions dwarf Bush's 'dangerous' spending,'* Byron York wrote that Bush started with a Clinton–era surplus of $128 billion in fiscal year 2001. Bush then had the following deficits:

- $158 billion in 2002
- $378 billion in 2003
- $413 billion in 2004
- $318 billion in 2005
- $248 billion in 2006
- $162 billion in 2007
- $410 billion in 2008

During the 8 years of the Bush administration, the national debt rose from $5 to $10 trillion. Based upon Obama's own budget projections, we will have annual deficits of $1 trillion for the next 10 years, doubling our national debt from $10 to $20 trillion by 2020.

Of all of our presidents in the past 50 years, Democratic President Bill Clinton will probably be remembered in history as one of our more fiscally conservative.

But What About the Poor?

"We should make the poor uncomfortable and kick them out of poverty" — Benjamin Franklin

In the April 7, 2010 Real Clear Politics story, *What am I*, John Stossel describes what it means to be a libertarian. Just like Thomas Jefferson, Stossel suggests that libertarians do not want government intrusion in their lives and want to be free in their pursuits. But could a libertarian system be unfair to the poor?

Another libertarian, Harvard economics instructor Jeffrey Miron, thinks that our current system harms the poor and punishes taxpayers by taking money away from those that work and giving it to those who don't. Miron feels that in a true libertarian system, workers would be treated more fairly and people in need would receive help from charities, not from the government. This would reduce the feeling of entitlement that many of the poor have today.

Stossel sites Wendy McElroy, founder of ifeminists.com, who feels that poor people's dependence on government aid stifles their drive and desire to better themselves.

Stossel also sites David Boaz, exec. V.P. of the Cato Institute. Boaz suggests that our country is rich and successful because of libertarian principles of individualism, free markets and private property ownership. Additionally, family support and self–help cooperatives enabled people to get themselves out of poverty in the 1930's. But Welfare and the Great Society programs have had the opposite affect of their intended goals. They have instead fostered government dependency, which inevitably harms the poor.

In the April 19, 2010 Real Clear Politics story, *Tea Partiers Fight Culture of Dependence*, Michael Barone suggests that public policy can either help or harm U.S. citizens. Obama and the

Democrats feel that government can do a better job and make better decisions than individuals. For example, government guarantees incomes through labor unions and healthcare through government programs, in other words, people are much better off under a culture of government dependence.

In the April 21, 2010 Real Clear Politics story, *Myths About Capitalism,* John Stossel questioned Michael Medved concerning myths about capitalism, for example, 'when the rich get richer, the poor get poorer.' Medved disagreed with this myth, suggesting instead that in most cases, when people engage in business, both must profit or they would not have engaged in the transaction in the first place. Medved calls this a 'double thank you.' Creating wealth doesn't cause poverty. Our current economic downturn suggests the opposite, that when the rich get poorer, everyone else does as well.

Heather MacDonald of the Manhattan Institute's City Journal, wrote that after 7 million lost jobs, crime is at its lowest levels in nearly five decades. This disproves the 'poverty causes crime' rationale for 1960's Great Society era expansion of social services.

MacDonald pointed out that crime fell during the Great Depression, but despite costly big–government programs, rose during the 1960s. Today's crime decline began amid the much better 1990's economy, and continues largely because of statistics–based, prevention–focused policing, which considers public safety a prerequisite for urban prosperity, and results in increased criminal incarceration.

MacDonald states that this proves that enforcing the rule of law makes the public safer, but warns that cutting police and releasing inmates early to save money is 'self–defeating.' Instead, cost savings should come from de–funding those 1960s–style

Welfare programs, their underlying premise which is now undeniably baseless.

In the June 2, 2010 Real Clear Politics story, *Were Liberals Wrong on Crime?* Richard Cohen wrote that conservatives may have been correct, that crime is committed by criminals and not caused by economic downturns or lack of employment. Cohen cites statistics from 2008 to 2009 that violent crime was down 5.5 percent overall and almost 7 percent in big cities. In Detroit, for instance, with the auto industry shedding workers, violent crime was down 2.4 percent. In Washington, D.C., murder was down 23.1 percent, rape 19.4 percent, and property crime 6 percent. Even in Phoenix with the rise in illegal immigration, violent crime was down almost 17 percent.

Cohen argues that everyday people do not go into a life of crime because they've been laid off or their home is worth less than their mortgage. The latest crime statistics strongly suggest that bad times do not necessarily make bad people, but instead, bad character makes bad people.

Government attempts to assist the poor have caused more harm than good. Social programs have done a huge disservice to the poor, often times locking them into reliance and dependency upon the government instead of encouraging and promoting self–reliance. ObamaCare is a perfect example. Why should I bother to work hard and earn money if the government will simply give me what I need for free, such as free or low cost healthcare? In other words, a government nanny–state removes the incentives for self–reliance.

The Problems with Congress

> *"There is danger from all men. The only maxim of a free government ought to be to trust no man living with power to endanger the public liberty" — John Adams*

In the April 5, 2010 Forbes story, *Liar, Liar,* Karlyn Bowman, senior fellow of the American Enterprise Institute, described the following polling data taken from both Democrats and Republicans

- In 1943, 69 percent said they wouldn't want their child to choose politics as a career, which was 63 percent in 1995.
- In 1943, nearly 48 percent polled said that it was almost impossible for a man to stay honest if he goes into politics, which rose to 55 percent by 1997.
- In 2006, 44 percent said that members of congress were more dishonest than most people.
- In 2010, only 9 percent described the ethical standards of congress as high and 55 percent said that it was low or very low, the only time a majority has given that response since the question was first asked in 1976.
- In 2010, 67 percent thought that elected officials were more interested in power and wealth than in public service for their constituents.

According to an April 19, 2010 Associated Press story, *Poll: Trust in Big Government Near Historic Low*

> In a Pew Research Center poll, nearly 80 percent of Americans say they can't trust Washington. Public confidence in the federal government is at one of the lowest points in a half century. Nearly half say the government negatively affects their daily lives, a sentiment that has grown over the past dozen years.
>
> *"The government's been lying to people for years. Politicians make promises to get elected, and when they get elected, they don't follow through,"* says Cindy Wanto, 57, a regis-

tered Democrat from Pennsylvania who joined several thousand for a rally in Washington on April 15. *"There's too much government in my business"*

Majorities in the survey call Washington too big and too powerful, and say it's interfering too much in state and local matters. *"I want an honest government. This isn't an honest government. It hasn't been for some time,"* said self–described independent David Willms, 54, of Florida. He faulted the White House and Congress under both parties.

Congressional members have become a huge problem for our nation. Over the years, they have arrogantly voted themselves pay and retirement benefit increases to the point where they are now in the top 5 percent of all U.S. wage earners. The average member of congress makes $172,000 plus about $40,000 in benefits, in addition to a huge retirement pension and 'Cadillac' benefits for the rest of their lives.

Congress has also increased the average annual federal employee wage, which is currently at about $70,000 plus about $40,000 in benefits, more than twice that of the average American wage and benefits (which is about $40,000 plus about $11,000 in benefits). Many of the higher paid federal employees in Washington make four times more than the average American.

Nancy A. Erickson is the Secretary of the Senate, an Executive Office, but still considered a Congressional Staffer. When she was hired on 01/04/07, her position paid $39,560. Two years later on 04/01/09, her salary was $87,229, a $47,668.34 increase in pay. Secretary Erickson more than doubled her pay in 2 years. In comparison, President Obama proposed only a 1.4 percent pay increase for the military, the lowest since 1973.

This is simply outrageous. We pay their salaries and they make considerably more than us. Perhaps this can be understood in the context of a quote from Glenn Beck, when he said that perhaps government workers are paid twice as much because it takes them twice as long to do their work.

A terrific quote comes from the 1984 movie Ghostbusters, which demonstrates the difference between working in the private and public sectors. After the main characters lose their jobs as university professors, Dr. Raymond Stantz (Dan Aykroyd) says *"We didn't have to produce anything. You don't know what it's like out there. I've worked in the private sector — they expect results."* Many government officials have never worked in the private sector, and don't understand what it means to be forced to work hard and meet or exceed the rigorous expectations set by others.

Congressional members have stacked the deck in such a way as to almost guarantee a job for life. Some members have even held office longer than many world monarchs and dictators. Libyan leader Muammar Qaddafi has only been in power 41 years, compared to Senator, Daniel K Inouye (D–HI) and Robert C Byrd (D–WV) who have been in the U.S. Congress for 50 and 56 years, respectively.

Here are statistics on the 111th Senate that were collected at the congressional website:

https://bioguide.congress.gov/biosearch/biosearch.asp

Age When First Elected to Senate

Younger than 45:	46%
45 to 55:	35%
55 to 59:	10%
60 to 64:	6%
Older than 64:	3%

Age Rages of Current Sitting Senators

Younger than 50:	7%
50 to 59:	29%
60 to 69:	35%
70 to 79:	24%
Older than 79:	5%

Current Senator Age Ranges

Min. age	41
Avg. age	63.99
Max. age	93

Current Avg. Number of Years in Senate: 17

Members who Have Served in Both houses

Both houses	45%
Average # of years	22.6
Average age	65.4
Max years served	56

Number of 6 year Senate Terms Served (Totals Years)	
Less than 1 term	22%
Between 1 and 3:	38%
Between 3 and5:	27%
Between 5 and 6:	10%
1 member has served	6.3 terms (38 years)
1 member has served	8.3 terms (50 years)
1 member has served	9.3 terms (56 years)

"Guests, like fish, begin to smell after three days" – Benjamin Franklin

Congressional members are also like fish, but many stink after only 2 terms. If it's unconstitutional to allow our President to serve more than 2 terms (8 years), why is it permissible for members of congress to serve up to 56 years, or longer?

After being elected, our representatives immediately begin working on getting re–elected. They raise millions of dollars from lobbyists and special interest groups (individuals and groups who will demand payback) and have created rules and regulations that hinder challengers. Look up 'gerrymandering' for your local congressional districts if you want to see some of the outrageous lengths they will go to in order to retain power. Unrelated earmarks and pork–barrel spending, neatly hidden within legislation, are nothing more than using 'your' money (or the money congress borrowed from China in your name) to bribe their electorate. And of course, there's the 'old–boy network:' *"…and if I vote for your pork–barrel spending, I expect you to vote for my pork– barrel spending in return."*

"A house divided against itself cannot stand" — Abraham Lincoln

Some Americans find it amusing when they see the partisan name–calling and infighting within congress. This behavior may have been laughable on a reality talk show, but it's unacceptable when it comes to the serious job of running of our country. Having a balance of well–mannered leaders from various political backgrounds seems to work well in keeping policy mostly in the middle where it represents the majority of our citizens. But it's a huge waste of our time and resources when the outcome of infighting and partisanship is gridlock and legislation that nobody wants. It's also embarrassing and unacceptable when our leaders behave like intolerant playground bullies, treating one another, and even the American people, with blatant intolerance, lacking in both civility and respect.

> *"When plunder becomes a way of life for a group of men living together in society, they create for themselves in the course of time a legal system that authorizes it and a moral code that justifies it" – Frederic Bastiat*

When congress voted on the 2,400+ page healthcare legislation, both the President and most members had not actually written or had even bothered to read the entire bill. Congressman John Conyers (D–MI) stated *"I love these members, they get up and say, 'Read the bill.' What good is reading the bill if it's a thousand pages and you don't have two days and two lawyers to find out what it means after you read the bill?"*

This kind of irresponsibility and even downright corruption is contagious. It is shown through the example of another Conyers, Ex–Detroit Councilwoman Monica Conyers. Monica Conyers, Rep. John Conyers' wife, was sentenced on March 3, 2010 by a federal judge to three years and one month in prison in a city corruption and bribery case. This illustrates just how desperately we need responsible leaders in our country.

However, this irresponsibility isn't limited to mere representatives and lower level government officials. In the May 06, 2010

National Review story, *Finding Out What's In It,* Yuval Levin writes

> In pressing for passage of the Democrats' massive and unpopular healthcare bill earlier this spring, Nancy Pelosi made the unorthodox argument that *"we have to pass the bill so that you can find out what is in it, away from the fog of the controversy."*

And as the fog lifts, you must be asking yourself 'Why again are members of congress in the top 5 percent of U.S. wage earners?' Frankly, this is criminal behavior. It's deplorable to push through an earmark filled, pork–laden, mind numbingly long, legally complex legislation that neither our representatives, nor the American people, have read or fully understand. Yet this legislation will have a monumental impact upon our nation's healthcare system and upon each citizen's personal health and finances.

In comparison to the healthcare legislative behemoth, the number of pages in the U.S. Constitution and in President Eisenhower's 1950's legislation that created the nationwide Interstate Highway System, are both less than 10 pages in length.

In the May 03, 2010 CommentaryMagazine.com story, *The Global Reform Dodge,* John Steele Gordon wrote that if the 1913 personal income tax law could be written in only 14 pages, why was ObamaCare over 2,400 pages and the financial reform bill about 1,400 pages?

Gordon wonders why major congressional bills are turning into unreadable, mind–numbing, legalese behemoths. He concludes that the goal is to actually make them 'unreadable.'

> Nancy Pelosi's now famous remark that congress would have to pass the healthcare bill before people

could know what was in it was more true than she realized. The political elite are confident that the Washington press corps won't go to the trouble of actually reading the huge bills.

A vast bill makes it easier to sneak in clauses that go unnoticed. If the best place to hide a book is in a library, then the best way to hide a favor for a contributor or a quiet little power grab is in a 2,000–page bill. The Washington Post recently reported that the financial reform bill would significantly increase the power of the Federal Trade Commission to regulate the Internet, something that has nothing to do with financial reform.

In the 1974 movie *Blazing Saddles,* when discussing the criminal problems occurring in the town of Rockridge, Governor William J. Le Petomane (Mel Brooks) states to his cabinet members *"We have to protect our phony baloney jobs here, gentlemen. We must do something about this immediately. Immediately. Immediately. Harrumph. Harrumph. Harrumph."*

This is exactly what our government does; protect their phony baloney jobs. We need to rein–in our out of control congress. It's time to shackle their unethical behaviors with the chains of the Constitution and kick them out of their phony baloney jobs.

Accountability and Lawbreakers

Has Senator Christopher Dodd (D–CT) or Rep. Barney Frank (D–MA) ever apologized for their active roles in the recent bursting of the housing bubble and our economy's financial meltdown? No, but they were more than happy to blame everyone else. And while these congressmen (and other federal officials) vilified private sector financial managers for receiving 'legal' pay bonuses, they said nothing about the huge executive pay bonuses given out by two financial companies closely tied to the congressmen: Fannie Mae and Freddie Mac.

According to an April 20, 2010 Wall Street Journal story, *Fannie and Freddie Amnesia,* Peter J. Wallison writes

> Fannie Mae and Freddie Mac bailout costs will reach $381 billion, the source of the greatest taxpayer losses.
>
> In July 2005, the Republican controlled Senate Banking Committee adopted tough regulatory legislation on a party line vote. The full Senate took no action because none of the 45 Democrats, including then Senator Barack Obama, voted in favor. If the bill had been enacted, many if not all of Fannie and Freddie losses might have been avoided.
>
> Obama stated in his April 2010 radio address that his financial regulatory proposals were struggling in the Senate because *"the financial industry and its powerful lobby have opposed modest safeguards against the kinds of reckless risks and bad practices that led to this very crisis."*
>
> Obama should know. As a senator, he was the third largest recipient of campaign contributions from Fannie and Freddie.

According to www.opensecrets.org, here is a breakdown of Fannie Mae and Freddie Mac's 1989 – 2008 campaign contributions to Congressional Democrats and Republicans:

Contribution Ranges	# Reps	Reps Total	# Dems	Dems Total	Grand Totals
$250 – $15k	100	$428k	157	$692k	**$1,119k**
$15k – $30k	25	$516k	30	$635k	**$1,151k**
$30k – $165k	18	$1,102k	24	$1,472	**$2,574k**
Grand Totals	**143**	**$2,046k**	**211**	**$2,799k**	k=$1,000

With billions of dollars and the bursting of the housing bubble at stake, how can we allow our congressional members to accept tens of thousands of dollars from the very organizations that they are tasked with regulating? This is a blatant conflict of interest. Here are some of the top Fannie and Freddie campaign contribution recipients, with Senator Christopher Dodd (D–CT) at the top of the list at $165,400. See if you recognize any of theses names:

Democrat	**Republican**
Dodd, Christopher J	Bennett, Robert F
Obama, Barack	Bachus, Spencer
Kerry, John	Blunt, Roy
Reed, Jack	Bond, Christopher S 'Kit'
Reid, Harry	Shelby, Richard C
Clinton, Hillary	Davis, Tom
Pelosi, Nancy	Boehner, John
Emanuel, Rahm	Reynolds, Tom
Frank, Barney	Pryce, Deborah
Bayh, Evan	Isakson, Johnny
Rangel, Charles B	McConnell, Mitch

As quoted in the above Wall Street Journal story, the government's cost to bail out Fannie and Freddie will eventually reach almost $400 billion dollars. And yet, it 'only' cost Fannie and Freddie less than $5 million in campaign contributions to pay–off our now President, the Speakers of the House and Senate, and some of the most influential leaders in the White House and Congress. What a terrific return on investment for Fannie and Freddie: 800,000 to 1.

According to the nonpartisan CQ MoneyLine, from January to March 2010 lobbyists spent an average $305 million a month to influence federal policy, more than double the monthly rate of spending in 2000.

In the May 10, 2010 Weekly Standard story, *Don't expect real reform from the Wall Street Democrats,* Christopher Caldwell writes

> *"Now, the Senate Republican leader, he paid a visit to Wall Street a week or two ago,"* said President Obama at a California fundraiser for Barbara Boxer in mid–April, putting on a mocking, homespun voice. *"He took along the chairman of their campaign committee. He met with some of the movers and shakers up there. I don't know exactly what was discussed. All I can tell you is when he came back, he promptly announced he would oppose the financial regulatory reform."*
>
> To judge from the guffawing that followed, few in attendance realized that Obama is more dependent on 'movers and shakers' in the financial sector than any president of our time, although the files of the Federal Election Commission make this clear as day. The movers at Goldman Sachs, whose top employees were grilled before the Senate Banking Committee last week, gave Obama's party three times as much money in the last cycle ($4.5 million) as they gave to Mitch McConnell's party ($1.5 million). The shakers at Citicorp gave Democrats almost twice as much ($3.1 million) as they gave to Republicans ($1.8 million).

Examining the campaign contributions from just Fannie, Freddie and Wall Street should prompt any casual observer to question whether there is way too much money in politics. Can the voice and will of the people ever be heard over the roaring influence of corporate contributions and Washington's money counting tables?

President Obama's cabinet and congress are riddled with former lobbyists, tax cheats and lawbreakers. Can the average citizen break our tax laws without consequence? No, but the United States Secretary of the Treasury, Timothy Geithner, easily got away with breaking our tax laws. But Geithner is in good company with other tax evading Obama cabinet members and appointees:

- Health and Human Services Secretary, Gov. Kathleen Sebelius
- The President's first HHS nominee, Tom Daschle
- Chief Performance Officer nominee, Nancy Killefer
- U.S. Trade Representative, Ron Kirk
- Labor Secretary, Hilda Solis

It would appear that these Obama officials enjoy championing and endorsing higher taxes, just as long as they don't personally have to pay their taxes.

In the October 9, 2009, CBS News story, *House Committee To Expand Rangel Investigation,* Marcia Kramer reported that the House Ethics Committee was expanding its investigation into embattled New York Congressman Charlie Rangel (D–NY).

> Rangel's sudden recollection this summer of at least $500,000 in cash assets and tens of thousands of dollars of investment income has gotten him into more hot water.

The House Ethics Committee is now going to investigate those 'memory lapses' as part of a probe that has already lasted 16 months (since June 2008).

The committee dropped a bombshell – it has so far issued 150 subpoenas, interviewed 34 witnesses, and analyzed 12,000 pages of documents relating to Rangel's affairs.

The evidence of Rangel's corruption is particularly damning. The March 3, 2010 USA Today story, *Rep. Rangel says he'll step down for now as Ways and Means chairman*, Catalina Camia and Fredreka Schouten wrote

> Rep. Charles Rangel said today he will temporarily step down as chairman of the powerful House Ways and Means Committee as an ethics panel continues an investigation of his activities. Last week, Rangel was admonished by the House Ethics Committee for taking trips to the Caribbean that were paid for by private companies — a violation of House gift rules.

Further evidence of the corruption in our government can be shown in the October 30, 2009 Washington Post story, *Dozens in Congress under ethics inquiry*, where Ellen Nakashima and Paul Kane reported that

> House ethics investigators have been scrutinizing the activities of more than 30 lawmakers and several aides in inquiries about issues including defense lobbying and corporate influence peddling, according to a confidential House ethics committee report prepared in July.

While you should keep these in mind, you shouldn't forget the backroom real estate deals by the likes of Senator Christopher Dodd (D–CT), or the 1997 campaign contributions that the DNC (Democratic National Committee) illegally accepted from China. Also remember that Senator Ted Stevens (R–AK) and Rep. Rick Renzi (R–AZ) were both caught up in F.B.I. corruption investigations, and Rep. William J. Jefferson's (D–LA) was caught with his freezer filled with $90,000 of bribe money; 'Hard Cold Cash.'

The Citizens for Responsibility and Ethics in Washington or 'CREW', publishes a list each year of the 'Most corrupt members of Congress,' that can be viewed at:

www.crewsmostcorrupt.org

In the April 26, 2010 McClatchy Newspapers story, *Obama energy official has ties to firms that stand to benefit,* Steven Thomma writes

> A top Obama administration official, who's helping lead a campaign for energy conservation, has a major financial interest in two companies that are poised to benefit from government spending.
>
> Cathy Zoi, once a close ally of former Vice President Al Gore, is the assistant secretary of energy for energy efficiency and renewable energy. She owns between $250,000 and $500,000 of stock in Landis+Gyr, a manufacturer of special electric meters used to create a 'smart grid.'
>
> Zoi's husband owns options on at least 120,000 shares of Serious Materials (and receives options on an additional 2,500 shares every month), a leading manufacturer of energy efficient windows praised by both Obama and Biden.

Ethics committees have a history of glacially slow rulings that typically amount to nothing more than a ceremonial slap on the offender's wrist. We can no longer allow or afford to have government officials police themselves, because they simply don't and won't.

It's time for our elected and appointed government officials to actually apologize for their mistakes and lawbreaking and to be held legally, financially and personally accountable for their actions, inactions and abuses.

Our Voices Must be Heard

In the March 25, 2010 Washington Times story, *'Go for it,' Obama tells GOP on health repeal,* Darlene Superville writes

> President Barack Obama dared Republicans to try to repeal his new health care law, telling them Thursday to *"Go for it and see how well they do with voters in November. Be my guest,"* Obama said in the first of many planned appearances to sell the revamp before fall congressional elections. *"If they want to have that fight, we can have it. Because I don't believe the American people are going to put the insurance industry back in the driver's seat."*

This prompts a very important question from the American people: 'Who's in the driver's seat now?' Are we truly better off when government manages or even takes over private businesses? Have authoritarian takeovers of private industry ever created prosperity for the citizens living under communists, socialists, fascists or dictatorships? Are there any examples in U.S. history where a government takeover resulted in lower costs and improved products or services?

President Obama didn't just taunt the Republicans when he challenged them to 'just try and repeal' his new healthcare law, he also taunted the American people who, by over a 2 to 1 majority, have repeatedly shown that they do not want the new healthcare law.

The progressive movement promotes an elitist view that the intellectuals in power always know what's best for the people, and if the people disagree, and even resist, they arrogantly dismiss the collective will of the people because 'government is always smarter.' This is egotistical, tyrannical, and dangerous.

In the 1976 movie *Network,* Howard Beale states *"I'm as mad as hell, and I'm not going to take this anymore."* Are you mad as hell yet? How long will the American people tolerate the dishonesty and dishonorable behavior of our government officials? How long will we allow our representatives to borrow and spend us into oblivion?

In the 2000 movie *Gladiator,* General Maximus says to Roman Emperor Commodus *"The time for honoring yourself will soon be at an end."* With some of the lowest approval ratings in fifty years, the pent–up anger of the people will soon be displayed in voting booths across America. As President Obama and congress are voted out of office, the time for honoring themselves will finally be at an end as well.

Thomas Jefferson had much to say on the relation between government and the governed

> *"The spirit of resistance to government is so valuable on certain occasions that I wish it to be always kept alive. It will often be exercised when wrong, but better so than not to be exercised at all"*
>
> *"The price of freedom is eternal vigilance"*

"What country can preserve its liberties if its rulers are not warned from time to time that their people preserve the spirit of resistance?"

"When the people fear their government, there is tyranny; when the government fears the people, there is liberty"

It is time to resist the continued failures, bloated policies and ethical corruptions of our government. The government will fear and respect its people only when the people speak up and demand liberty over tyranny. It's time to 'Reclaim Liberty!'

This chapter was entitled with a slightly altered version of Patrick Henry's famous March 23, 1775 speech. So here at the end of this chapter, it must be quoted correctly

"Is life so dear, or peace so sweet, as to be purchased at the price of chains and slavery? Forbid it, Almighty God. I know not what course others may take; but as for me, give me Liberty or give me Death" — Patrick Henry

X – Take Back Our Government Now

Hope and Change?

We were promised Hope and Change in 2008, but the change isn't what we expected, and our nation is running out of hope (and money).

Perhaps we misunderstood candidate Obama who may have actually promised us 'hope of chains.' Let's consider Greek mythology for a moment. Just like the legend of Sisyphus, we too are currently cursed until the end of time, chained to an enormous financial boulder of debt that we are forced to roll up a very steep hill. As we roll it up that never ending slope, the boulder keeps growing larger and larger as the federal government continues to borrow and spend us deeper into debt. And throughout eternity, just as we reach that mythical hilltop where our terrible task will finally be brought to an end, the boulder rolls back to the bottom of the hill where we start all over again, rolling it back up.

Instead of allowing ourselves to be enslaved to this enormous ever–growing debt for all eternity, we can turn to Thomas Jefferson for a different 'hope of chains'

> *"The two enemies of the people are criminals and government, so let us tie the second down with the chains of the Constitution so the second will not become the legalized version of the first"*

Our vision of America should be more like the Greek tale of Daedalus and his son Icarus. Daedalus, a remarkable Athenian craftsman, made two pairs of wings out of wax and feathers so that he and his son could escape their exile by 'flying' away from Crete and King Minos. The sad moral of the story tells how Icarus became overwhelmed by the thrill of flying and ventured too close to the sun and perished.

Isn't it better to be free to use our creativity and drive as we see fit? To reach for the stars while pursuing liberty and prosperity seems much better than being trapped by tyranny, even if our goals and endeavors may end with failure. The right to try and fail is much better than being coddled and directed by an overpowering, unjust government.

"The policy of the American government is to leave their citizens free, neither restraining nor aiding them in their pursuits" – Thomas Jefferson

All Politics are Local

According to the former Speaker of the House, the late Tip O'Neill *"All politics are local."*

The American people cannot hope to make an impact on Washington if they haven't made one in their own backyard. We cannot expect our representatives to be truthful, honest, ethical and noble, if we're not willing to be so as well. We cannot truly love our country unless we first love ourselves, our family and our neighbors.

"A community is like a ship; everyone ought to be prepared to take the helm" – Henrik Ibsen

Be an active member of your community, informed about current local and national news. Make your voice heard. If your library doesn't filter pornographic websites from their public computers, then go to your city council meetings and ask them to start installing and using filters. If your local schools are teaching radical ideology, then go to the school board meetings and demand mainstream curriculum. If your mayor does something honorable that you agree with, write a letter to the editor of your local newspaper commending the admirable behavior.

Attend a local house of worship regularly. Get to know your neighbors and assist them when they need help. Give some of your resources to local charities and worthwhile organizations. Help out at charitable food banks and kitchens because the poor need hot meals throughout the year, not just on Thanksgiving and Christmas.

Vote the Bums Out

Register to vote and take an active role in elections, perhaps even volunteering at a polling location. Learn everything you can about your representatives, and especially your judges. Support candidates who respect the will of the people and are truthful, honest, ethical, noble and fiscally conservative. Also, do not forget that it is sometimes your representatives who appoint your judges.

There are some truly terrible judges in our country and you may have to stand before one of them someday. Some judges are prejudiced towards certain minority groups, gender or politically affiliations, and some simply do not uphold our laws. There are activist judges who try to make the laws themselves and 'compassionate' judges who are soft on criminals, at times only giving probation to loathsome child rapists. We need to focus our collective spotlights on these incompetent and corrupt judges and put an end to their careers on the bench.

Support Good Candidates

After you identify good candidates and leaders, support them. Knock on doors and tell your neighbors why they should vote for your candidate. Go to rallies, hold up signs, wave the American flag, put a bumper sticker on your vehicle and volunteer to make telephone calls in support of your candidates. Also, support their campaigns with financial donations. A good saying to remember is to 'put your money where your mouth is.'

Communication

Communicate with your representatives often to ensure that they understand the will and desires of their constituents. And when they misrepresent you and violate the will of the people, vote them out for a worthwhile replacement.

Over the years, I've know people who always vote against incumbents, whether they are or are not doing a good job. Their logic is to always vote against incumbents in order to keep politicians humble and deny them the time or opportunity to become comfortable and corrupt within their seat of power. I've also known people who always vote against tax increases, hoping that it will send a message and force government to streamline itself and live within its means. I'm not sure that these are the best strategies for voting, but they do send a powerful message about how voters view their representatives and the operations of government.

XI – Constitutional Amendments

Our founding fathers framed the Constitution with rights and constraints in order to create a sound and just republic. They also gave us the ability to modify the Constitution, but made the process challenging. This was done in order to safeguard the Constitution from abuse of power and from the fickle whims and passing fancies of the time.

According to Dr. Jonathan Mott of BYU's McKay School of Education

www.thisnation.com/textbook/constitution–features.html

> *A Flexible Document*
>
> The American Framers hoped, that the Constitution they were drafting would serve the nation for many decades; however, they would probably be pleasantly surprised to learn that it has now been in effect for more than two centuries. The success of the document is due in large part to the flexibility built into it. When changes have been necessary, the amendment process provided by the Constitution itself has been available. However, while the Constitution has been amended twenty–seven times, most of the changes made in the American political system have been made without formally amending the Constitution.
>
> Almost since the day it was ratified, the 'general welfare' clause in the Preamble and the 'necessary and proper' clause in Article I have been considered the 'penumbra' of the Constitution, that portion of the document that the framers purposely left for future generations to debate and define. It appears that in many instances, the framers were content to leave unanswered questions about what is 'Constitutional' and what is not.

For the Constitution to survive, they knew that it would have to be a living, breathing document, capable of both imposing order on the interactions of governments and people as well as reflecting their values and needs as times changed.

Here are some goals that might be achieved through new Constitutional amendments. See if you can come up with your own ideas and improve upon these suggestions:

- Balanced federal budgets
- Elimination of the national debt
- Elimination of federal borrowing and control of spending
- Regain and protect individual and States rights
- Fix or eliminate our progressive income tax
- Rein–in congress including congressional pay, term limits and ethical abuses
- Reform the legislative process
- Demand lawful, ethical, honest, transparent behavior from the federal government, and prosecute all violators

Please write down some of your ideas for fixing government:

____

____

____

____

____

____

____

"The greatest danger for most of us lies not in setting our aim too high and falling short, but in setting our aim too low, and achieving our mark" — Michelangelo

Here are some suggestions for new U.S. Constitutional Amendments:

1) Balanced federal budgets that do not exceed eighteen percent of GDP (currently at 60.4 percent), where no less than twenty percent of the federal budget, and all budget surpluses, will be used to repay government debt and financial obligations.

This amendment would limit the size of the federal government, tie its' spending directly to an important economic indicator, the GDP (or Gross Domestic Product), and would require the government to pay off its debts. (A foolproof standard would need to be established for calculating the GDP without risk of political manipulation.) During good economic times, the government would have more money to spend and during bad economic times, they would be forced to downsize and live within their means.

2) Rapid elimination of all federal debt and loans. We are currently paying over $400 billion per year on the interest of our national debt, with estimates of it increasing to $1.6 trillion by 2020. If our debts were eliminated, the money that we are currently paying on interest could be used for running the government and reducing taxes, instead of paying our creditors.

3) All federal borrowing approved by 2/3 vote by the States. This would remove the federal government's borrowing authority and place it instead into the hands of the states and the people. The federal government has repeatedly demonstrated a blatant disregard for the financial health of our nation by the massive, ever growing debt they have forced upon the backs of the American people.

4) All current and future programs and mandates will either be fully funded or eliminated. This would force the federal government to live within its means, just like most American families. Money collected for specific programs, such as Social Security, Medicare, federal road tax, could only be used for those specific programs and nowhere else. The moneys not use, i.e., federal road taxes, would be returned to the taxpayers.

5) Ensure that individual and States rights supersede federal laws that overreach / impede State's or individual's rights or that place unreasonable financial hardships on the States or upon individuals.

6) Elimination of the current progressive income tax, replaced by either a flat income tax or a consumption tax. All income related taxes could be eliminated and replaced by a consumption tax, such as a national sales tax. Imagine how wonderful it would be if you no longer had to fill out and submit long, confusing forms that contain some of your most personal information every April 15, and no longer faced the risk of being audited and abused by the IRS.

7) Repeal the seventeenth amendment, which would restore the original Constitutional procedures for selecting U.S. Senators. The seventeenth amendment was ratified on April 8, 1913 during President Woodrow Wilson's administration. The original intent of the founding fathers was to have the people elect their U.S. House Representatives by popular vote and to have Senators appointed by the states. The states lost their voices and important influences at the federal level in 1913 when Senators were no longer selected by the states and instead began to also be elected by popular vote of the people. Article V of the U.S. Constitution states *"that no State, without its Consent, shall be deprived of its equal Suffrage in the Senate."* It can be argued that the states were deprived (lost) their suffrage (right to vote) in the Senate after the ratification of the seventeenth amendment.

The seventeenth amendment also introduced the corrupting influences of campaign contributions and lobbyist money into the Senate selection process and a trend where Senators began to stay in office much longer. One example of the negative influences of money can be seen in the congressional campaigns of Christopher Dodd, Tommy Sowers, Rahm Emanuel, Lois Gutierrez, Bobby Rush, Jesse Jackson, Danny Davis and Jan Shakowsky (among others) who all received more campaign contributions from outside of their districts than from within. To whom exactly are their allegiances?

A Senator's allegiances are no longer to the states who would have appointed them prior to 1913. And now, their allegiances are not even to their constituents who elect them when they rely so heavely on moneys from outside of their districts to gain and remain in power.

8) Congressional term limits; 2–terms (12 years) for Senators and 3–terms (6 years) for House members, and no more than 12 years total for combined service in both the House and Senate.

Our founding fathers set personal examples of service to our country, limited their time in office, then returned home. Just like our twenty–second amendment to the Constitutional that enacted Presidential term limits after FDR, congressional term limits may also be needed to stop the practices of life long political careers.

If members cannot accomplish what they need to in 6 — 12 years, what are the chances they will accomplish anything monumental in 40 years or longer? When they retain office for such a long time they can become addicted to the power and prestige of the office and learn all the tricks of staying in office and manipulating the system, all the while protecting and scratching each other's backs. Our nation can no longer afford the burdens, the corruptions and the incompetence of career public office holders.

There are and have been very good, honorable congressmen and women who we'd hate to see leave prematurely. But it's outrageous to read the U.S. Senate's website list of the top 25 longest serving Senators (out of 100), from George Aiken (R–VT) 33+ years to Robert C. Byrd (D–WV) 50+ years.

One example of a long serving congressman would be John Kyl (R–AZ). After serving 24 years in both the House and Senate, most observers would agree that Senator Kyl has served with honor and distinction and brings a wealth of experience and maturity to congress. Perhaps a term limit system could allow a seasoned, respected Senator, like Kyl, to be kept on for a year or two after leaving office as a paid mentor who assists newly elected congressional members.

The 1994 Republican Revolution provided a hopeful view of how congress could operate with younger, less experienced members and more frequent turnover. The 1994 election brought in 54 new, young, inexperienced members to the House of Representatives. For the first time, these congressmen placed numerous restrictions and limits on themselves, which truly pleased their constituents. Congressional history typically hasn't shown this type of self–denying ethical behavior with longer serving members. The argument can be made that increasing the regularity of turnover may improve ethical behavior while bringing fresh new ideas to government.

If term limits are too extreme a solution, then perhaps other constraints could be enacted to make it difficult for congressional members to turn their government service into life long careers. In the Federalist No. 39 paper, James Madison offered this description of how our republican government would be " *administered by persons holding their offices during pleasure, for a limited period, or during good behavior.*"

Madison and other framers believed that our leaders should hold office for a limited period of time, by the pleasure of the people, and during the good behavior of those leaders. Solutions for limiting their time in office could include new rules where congressional members would be ineligible to run for re–election if their average district–wide constituent polling numbers had been below 50 percent (displeasure of the people), or if they have been convicted of violating laws or had broken government ethics rules (bad behaviors).

9) Establishment of independent, nonpartisan prosecutors. They would replace ethics committees, to ensure the legal and ethical conduct of elected and appointed government officials, and to vigorously prosecute all violators. No one is immune to or above the law.

10) End contributions and all influences of money in politics. Stop campaign contributions and the influences of special interest groups, organizations, corporations and paid lobbyists from federal politics. All meetings with federal officials would be video and audio recorded and easily available for public review. Federal officials who secretly meet with lobbyists could be fined $100 per minute.

11) Caps on Congressional and Federal employee salaries and benefits, directly tied to the average American salary. Congressional members' salaries and total compensation (including benefits) would not exceed two or three times the national average American salary, which is currently at about $40,000 per year plus about $11,000 in benefits.

Federal employee and contractor salaries plus their total compensation (including benefits) would not exceed the national average for a similar private sector job.

This would tie federal salaries and benefits to the amounts that typical Americans make, and would not allow government officials to arbitrarily vote pay raises for themselves or for other government employees.

12) Congressional legislation reform; all legislation must begin with a detailed list of it's enumerated powers and written proof that the legislation is Constitutional; must be written using language and structure whereas a high school graduate can easily read and understand; all laws apply equally to both the people and the government; caps on the length of legislation (i.e., 100 pages); a minimum amount of time (i.e., 30 days) that legislation must be available for public review prior to a vote; congressional members and the president must provide verifiable proof that they have read the entire bill before they can vote on it or sign it into law; no earmarks or pork–barrel spending could be included; no text or provisions unrelated to the overall purpose of each specific legislation could be included.

13) Establishment of a panel of nonpartisan Constitutional scholars to openly evaluate all federal legislation and procedures to ensure that they adhere to and do not violate the Constitution and the rights of the States and individuals.

14) Establishment of a National Voter Initiative whereby the people, through national referendums, can repeal bad federal laws, order congress to change it's fiscal policies, and control congressional behavior.

This suggested amendment is similar to provisions found in many states that allow their citizens to propose and vote on laws through a proposition or ballot initiative process. In this case, it would allow citizens, on a national level, to repeal bad legislation (i.e., ObamaCare) and rein–in congress. This would allow the people to directly reform the federal government without the need to amend the U.S. Constitution numerous times to achieve:

- Balanced federal budgets
- Limited federal spending / borrowing / debt limits
- Congressional pay and term limits
- Congressional ethical standards and punishments

This power does have potential problems. In California and elsewhere, special interest groups used the voter initiative process to successfully pass medical marijuana laws. These were nothing more than a backdoor way of legalizing an illegal drug. A national voter initiative system would need to have strong limits and safeguards:

- For use by the citizens only, and not for the use of special interest groups
- Set the required percentage of voters needed for passage rather high, for example, at 2/3 majority
- Only allow the national voter initiative to be used for repealing bad laws, not creating new laws. An initiative could also be used to 'direct' congress to create specific laws.
- To set standards of conduct and restrictions on government officials (i.e., congressional term limits, and limits on salaries and benefits.)

Another approach might be to provide the states or American citizens limited use of the 'Private right of action' where they could sue the federal government when laws or the actions of government officials violate their Constitutional rights.

Allowing direct elections would change our national political system, in this one specific area, from a republic to more of a direct democracy. Our founding fathers designed our nation as a republic, or representative form of government, mostly because they feared pure democracies and felt that they simply don't last, as had been the case throughout world history. To a lesser more practical degree, they may have also considered the limitations of slow communications, distances and isolation of many of its citizens and colonies when selecting a representative form of government. If eighteenth century travel and communications had been as robust as ours is today, or even that of the beginning of the twentieth century, then perhaps our founding fathers may have included some democratic elements into our republic.

15) Move the date of all National elections to April 16. This terrific idea was originally made by the political writer, Thomas Sowell. Just imagine how the people's vote would be influenced if it occurred the day after they had been forced to pay their income taxes.

The next chapter describes how to amend the U.S. Constitution. For many, this may seem like an extreme prescription for curing our nation's ills, but our government is hemorrhaging money and needs to be cured. State and citizen–sponsored Constitutional amendments may be the only way to fix our government and demonstrate the resolve of the American people, the majority of whom are fed up with the government.

In 1994, during the 104th session of Congress, the Republicans introduced the 'Contract with America.' During that 'Republican Revolution,' they were able to win control of congress, mostly in response to public anger directed at former President Clinton's attempt to pass healthcare reform (a.k.a., HillaryCare). Sound familiar?

There were a number of unfulfilled or short lived promises made in the Contract, including these:

- Requiring all laws apply equally to the congress
- A comprehensive audit of congress for waste, fraud or abuse

- Cutting the number of House committees and staff by 1/3
- Limiting the terms of all committee chairs
- Requiring committee meetings to be open to the public
- Requiring a three–fifths majority vote to pass a tax increase
- Guaranteeing an honest accounting of our federal budget

In the Contract, the Republicans also promised within the first 100 days to bring to the House floor ten bills. The first and most important bill in the list was 'The Fiscal Responsibility Act', which read:

"A balanced budget / tax limitation amendment and a legislative line–item veto to restore fiscal responsibility to an out of control Congress, requiring them to live under the same budget constraints as families and businesses."

The Republicans enjoyed a majority in congress for 12 years throughout the remainder of Clinton's Presidency and for the first 6 years of Bush's Presidency. Sixteen years later, where exactly is our promised Balanced Budget Amendment?

During the past 16 years, the American people could have truly benefited from these reforms if they had been made permanent, particularly the Balanced Budget Amendment, and especially now during our current out of control federal borrowing and spending. The lesson we need to learn from 1994 is that neither party in congress can be trusted to truly reform the federal government, or themselves.

What Do We do Next?

Now it's our turn. We must demand and facilitate changes to our government through:

- State Sponsored Constitutional Amendments (3/4 of the States to ratify)

- Voter Initiatives
- The Ballot Box
- Your Representatives
- The Media

Further Actions Include

- Voting the bums out, replaced with fiscal conservatives
- Getting involved in the political process at the local, state and national levels
- Attending, joining and supporting pro–Constitutional organizations such as the Tea Party movement
- Writing letters and calling your representatives and the media often
- Demanding honest, ethical, transparent behavior from your representatives and the political parties, or replace them
- Demanding a nonpartisan media

"The greatest pleasure in life is doing what people say you cannot do" – Walter Bagehot

Demand these changes, but remember that it is unlikely that the federal government will ever change itself willingly. God speed to you in your many endeavors to restore our Constitutional government, and to 'Reclaim Liberty!'

XII — How to Amend the U.S. Constitution

Article V of the U.S. Constitution:

The Congress, whenever two thirds of both Houses shall deem it necessary, shall propose Amendments to this Constitution, or, on the Application of the Legislatures of two thirds of the several States, shall call a Convention for proposing Amendments, which, in either Case, shall be valid to all Intents and Purposes, as Part of this Constitution, when ratified by the Legislatures of three fourths of the several States, or by Conventions in three fourths thereof, as the one or the other Mode of Ratification may be proposed by the Congress; Provided that no Amendment which may be made prior to the Year One thousand eight hundred and eight shall in any Manner affect the first and fourth Clauses in the Ninth Section of the first Article; and that no State, without its Consent, shall be deprived of its equal Suffrage in the Senate.

The following text was taken from:

http://www.usconstitution.net/

Amending the United States Constitution is no small task. This page will detail the amendment procedure as spelled out in the Constitution, and will also list some of the Amendments that have not been passed, as well as give a list of some amendments proposed in Congress during several of the past sessions.

The Amendment Process

There are essentially two ways spelled out in the Constitution for how to propose an amendment. One has never been used.

The first method is for a bill to pass both houses of the legislature, by a two–thirds majority in each. Once the bill has passed both houses, it goes on to the states. This is the route taken by all current amendments. Because of some long outstanding amendments, such as the 27th, Congress will normally put a time limit (typically seven years) for the bill to be approved as an amendment (for example, see the 21st and 22nd).

The second method prescribed is for a Constitutional Convention to be called by two–thirds of the legislatures of the States, and for that Convention to propose one or more amendments. These amendments are then sent to the states to be approved by three–fourths of the legislatures or conventions. This route has never been taken, and there is discussion in political science circles about just how such a convention would be convened, and what kind of changes it would bring about.

Regardless of which of the two proposal routes is taken, the amendment must be ratified, or approved, by three–fourths of states. There are two ways to do this, too. The text of the amendment may specify whether the bill must be passed by the state legislatures or by a state convention. See the Ratification Convention Page for a discussion of the make up of a convention. Amendments are sent to the legislatures of the states by default. Only one amendment, the 21st, specified a convention. In any case, passage by the legislature or convention is by simple majority.

The Constitution, then, spells out four paths for an amendment:

- Proposal by convention of states, ratification by state conventions (never used)
- Proposal by convention of states, ratification by state legislatures (never used)

- Proposal by Congress, ratification by state conventions (used once)
- Proposal by Congress, ratification by state legislatures (used all other times)

It is interesting to note that at no point does the President have a role in the formal amendment process (though he would be free to make his opinion known). He cannot veto an amendment proposal, nor a ratification. This point is clear in Article 5, and was reaffirmed by the Supreme Court in Hollingsworth v Virginia (3 U.S. 378 [1798]):

The negative of the President applies only to the ordinary cases of legislation: He has nothing to do with the proposition, or adoption, of amendments to the Constitution.

Informal Amendment

Another way the Constitution's meaning is changed is often referred to as 'informal amendment.' This phrase is a misnomer, because there is no way to informally amend the Constitution, only the formal way. However, the meaning of the Constitution, or the interpretation, can change over time.

There are two main ways that the interpretation of the Constitution changes, and hence its meaning. The first is simply that circumstances can change. One prime example is the extension of the vote. In the times of the Constitutional Convention, the vote was often granted only to moneyed land holders. Over time, this changed and the vote was extended to more and more groups. Finally, the vote was extended to all males, then all persons 21 and older, and then to all persons 18 and older. The informal status quo became law, a part of the Constitution, because that was the direction the culture was headed. Another example is the political process that has evolved in the United States: political parties, and their trappings (such as primaries and conventions) are not mentioned or contemplated in the Constitution, but they are fundamental to our political system.

The second major way the meaning of the Constitution changes is through the judiciary. As the ultimate arbiter of how the Constitution is interpreted, the judiciary wields more actual power than the Constitution alludes to. For example, before the Privacy Cases, it was perfectly Constitutional for a state to forbid married couples from using contraception; for a state to forbid blacks and whites to marry; to abolish abortion. Because of judicial changes in the interpretation of the Constitution, the nation's outlook on these issues changed.

In neither of these cases was the Constitution changed. Rather, the way we looked at the Constitution changed, and these changes had a far reaching effect. These changes in meaning are significant because they can happen by a simple judge's ruling and they are not a part of the Constitution and so they can be changed later.

Popular Amendment

One other way of amendment is also not mentioned in the Constitution, and, because it has never been used, is lost on many students of the Constitution. Framer James Wilson, however, endorsed popular amendment, and the topic is examined at some length in Akhil Reed Amar's book, The Constitution: A Biography.

The notion of popular amendment comes from the conceptual framework of the Constitution. Its power derives from the people; it was adopted by the people; it functions at the behest of and for the benefit of the people. Given all this, if the people, as a whole, somehow demanded a change to the Constitution, should not the people be allowed to make such a change? As Wilson noted in 1787, '... the people may change the Constitutions whenever and however they please. This is a right of which no positive institution can ever deprive them.'

It makes sense — if the people demand a change, it should be made. The change may not be the will of the Congress, nor of the states, so the two enumerated methods of amendment might not be practical, for they rely on these institutions. The real issue is not in the conceptual. It is a reality that if the people do not support the Constitution in its present form, it cannot survive. The real issue is in the practical. Since there is no process specified, what would the process be? There are no national elections today — even elections for the presidency are local. There is no precedent for a national referendum. It is easy to say that the Constitution can be changed by the people in any way the people wish. Actually making the change is another story altogether.

Suffice it to say, for now, that the notion of popular amendment makes perfect sense in the Constitutional framework, even though the details of effecting popular amendment could be impossible to resolve.

XIII — Important Quotes from Our American Founding Fathers, Great Leaders and Thinkers:

"Yesterday the greatest question was decided which ever was debated in America; and a greater perhaps never was, nor will be, decided among men. A resolution was passed without one dissenting colony, that these United Colonies are, and of right ought to be, free and independent States" — John Adams

Protecting Freedom

"The price of freedom is eternal vigilance" — Thomas Jefferson

"They who can give up essential liberty to obtain a little temporary safety, deserve neither liberty nor safety" — Benjamin Franklin

"What country can preserve its liberties if its rulers are not warned from time to time that their people preserve the spirit of resistance?" – Thomas Jefferson

"The spirit of resistance to government is so valuable on certain occasions that I wish it to be always kept alive. It will often be exercised when wrong, but better so than not to be exercised at all" — Thomas Jefferson

"When the people fear their government, there is tyranny; when the government fears the people, there is liberty" — Thomas Jefferson

"The two enemies of the people are criminals and government, so let us tie the second down with the chains of the Constitution so the second will not become the legalized version of the first" — Thomas Jefferson

"America will never be destroyed from the outside. If we falter and lose our freedoms, it will be because we destroyed ourselves" — Abraham Lincoln

"The course of history shows that as government grows, liberty decreases" — Thomas Jefferson

"A house divided against itself cannot stand" — Abraham Lincoln

"I deem one of the essential principles of our government... equal and exact justice to all men of whatever state or persuasion, religious or political" — Thomas Jefferson

"I always consider the settlement of America with reverence and wonder, as the opening of a grand scene and design in providence, for the illumination of the ignorant and the emancipation of the slavish part of mankind all over the earth" — John Adams

"In a free and republican government, you cannot restrain the voice of the multitude; every man will speak as he thinks, or more properly without thinking" — George Washington

"I consider the people who constitute a society or a nation as the source of all authority in that nation" — Thomas Jefferson

"There is danger from all men. The only maxim of a free government ought to be to trust no man living with power to endanger the public liberty" — John Adams

"Facts are stubborn things; and what ever may be our wishes, our inclinations, or the dictates of our passions, they can not alter the state of facts, and evidence" — John Adams

Government Intrusion

"The democracy will cease to exist when you take away from those who are willing to work and give to those who would not" — Thomas Jefferson

"Fear is the foundation of most governments" — John Adams

"I predict future happiness for Americans if they can prevent the government from wasting the labors of the people under the pretense of taking care of them" — Thomas Jefferson

"The policy of the American government is to leave their citizens free, neither restraining nor aiding them in their pursuits" — Thomas Jefferson

"The proposition that the people are the best keepers of their own liberties is not true. They are the worst conceivable, they are no keepers at all; they can neither judge, act, think, or will, as a political body" — John Adams

"To take from one because it is thought that his own industry and that of his father's has acquired too much, in order to spare to others, who, or whose fathers, have not exercised equal industry and skill, is to violate arbitrarily the first principle of association–the guarantee to every one of a free exercise of his industry and the fruits acquired by it" – Thomas Jefferson

"Everyone has a natural right to choose that vocation in life which he thinks most likely to give him comfortable subsistence" — Thomas Jefferson

"It is not everyone who asketh that deserveth charity; all however, are worth of the inquiry or the deserving may suffer" — George Washington

"All the perplexities, confusion and distress in America arise, not from defects in their Constitution or Confederation, not from want of honor or virtue, so much as from the downright ignorance of the nature of coin, credit and circulation" — John Adams

"When plunder becomes a way of life for a group of men living together in society, they create for themselves in the course of time a legal system that authorizes it and a moral code that justifies it" — Frederic Bastiat

Faith, Honor, Family

"The propitious smiles of Heaven can never be expected on a nation that disregards the eternal rules of order and right which Heaven itself has ordained" — George Washington

"I hope that I shall always possess firmness and virtue enough to maintain what I consider to be the most enviable of all titles, the character of an honest man" — George Washington

"It is in the love of one's family only that heartfelt happiness is known. By a law of our nature, we cannot be happy without the endearing connections of a family" — Thomas Jefferson

"A desire to be observed, considered, esteemed, praised, beloved, and admired by his fellows is one of the earliest as well as the keenest dispositions discovered in the heart of man" — John Adams

"Arms in the hands of citizens may be used at individual discretion... in private self–defense" — John Adams

Truth

"Men occasionally stumble over the truth, but most of them pick themselves up and hurry off as if nothing ever happened" — Sir Winston Churchil

Unions

"Government employee unions are a pestilence, a plague. They're worst than the baddest locust swarm you've ever imagined ...though not nearly as smart and hard working. Oh ... and government employee unions eat taxpayer money instead of crops" — Neal Boortz

Democracy

"Democracy is the only system that persists in asking the powers that be whether they are the powers that ought to be" — Sydney J. Harris, American journalist and author

Honesty:

"I hope that I shall always possess firmness and virtue enough to maintain what I consider to be the most enviable of all titles, the character of an honest man" — George Washington

Marriage and Family:

"It is in the love of one's family only that heartfelt happiness is known. By a law of our nature, we cannot be happy without the endearing connections of a family" — Thomas Jefferson

Justice:

"I deem one of the essential principles of our government... equal and exact justice to all men of whatever state or persuasion, religious or political" — Thomas Jefferson

Life, Liberty, and The Pursuit of Happiness:

"Everyone has a natural right to choose that vocation in life which he thinks most likely to give him comfortable subsistence" — Thomas Jefferson

Charity:

"It is not everyone who asketh that deserveth charity; all however, are worth of the inquiry or the deserving may suffer" — George Washington

On your right to disagree:

"In a free and republican government, you cannot restrain the voice of the multitude; every man will speak as he thinks, or more properly without thinking" — George Washington

Who works for whom?

"I consider the people who constitute a society or a nation as the source of all authority in that nation" — Thomas Jefferson

XIV — Patriotic Songs

The Battle Hymn to Reclaim Liberty

(Sung to: The Battle Hymn of the Republic[A]*)*

By Robert J. Thorpe, original last stanza by Julia Ward Howe

Mine eyes have seen the promise, of the coming Liberty,
As our Founders hath bestowed, upon our land of Brave and Free,[1]
With Eagle's[B] wings extended, we will fly to victory,
The People are marching on.

Glory. Glory. Hallelujah. Glory. Glory. Hallelujah.
Glory. Glory. Hallelujah. The People are marching on.

Our Boston Tea Party, fought tyranny on the waves,
Then Patriots fighting Red Coats, many died our noble brave,
Again we struggle for justice, force our leaders to behave,[2]
The Patriots are marching on.

Glory. Glory. Hallelujah. Glory. Glory. Hallelujah.
Glory. Glory. Hallelujah. The Patriots are marching on.

As government grows larger, tyranny grows right along,[3]
Traded freedom in for safety, in a heartbeat both were gone,[4]
Just try to mute the people, loud resistance is our song,[5]
Our Nation is marching on.

Glory. Glory. Hallelujah. Glory. Glory. Hallelujah.
Glory. Glory. Hallelujah. Our Nation is marching on.

Restoring our Republic, oh the changes we will see,
Constitutional adherence, will set the people free,[6]
A government restrained, is ordained for Liberty,[7]
The Tea Party is marching on.

Glory. Glory. Hallelujah. Glory. Glory. Hallelujah.
Glory. Glory. Hallelujah. The Tea Party is marching on.

Mine eyes have seen the glory, of the coming of the Lord,[8]
He is trampling out the vintage, where the grapes of wrath are stored,
He has loosed the fateful lightening, of His terrible swift sword,
His truth is marching on.

Glory. Glory. Hallelujah. Glory. Glory. Hallelujah.
Glory. Glory. Hallelujah. His truth is marching on.

[1]*"I know not what course others may take; but as for me, give me liberty or give me death!" — Patrick Henry*

[2]*"What country can preserve its liberties if its rulers are not warned from time to time that their people preserve the spirit of resistance?" – Thomas Jefferson*

[3]*"The course of history shows that as government grows, liberty decreases" – Thomas Jefferson*

[4]*"They who can give up essential liberty to obtain a little temporary safety, deserve neither liberty nor safety" – Benjamin Franklin*

[5]*"When the people fear their government, there is tyranny; when the government fears the people, there is liberty" – Thomas Jefferson*

[6]*"The two enemies of the people are criminals and government, so let us tie the second down with the chains of the Constitution so the second will not become the legalized version of the first" – Thomas Jefferson*

[7]*"I consider the people who constitute a society or a nation as the source of all authority in that nation" – Thomas Jefferson*

[8]*"The propitious smiles of Heaven can never be expected on a nation that disregards the eternal rules of order and right which Heaven itself has ordained" – from George Washington's first Inaugural address*

[A]Although *The Battle Hymn of the Republic* was written during the Civil War, the context is appropriate here because once again, we are struggling against domestic tyranny, not foreign oppression.

[B]On the morning when I began writing these lyrics, an American Bald Eagle flew up our mountaintop forest driveway, about 20 feet above the ground, flying about 50 feet away when it passed by me. Breathtaking! I'm not sure if this experience had an ordained spiritual significance, but I thank God, nonetheless, for that rich, patriotic blessing.

Our National Anthem, The Star Spangled Banner

By Francis Scott Key 1814

Oh, say can you see, by the dawn's early light
What so proudly we hailed, at the twilight's last gleaming?
Whose broad stripes and bright stars, thru the perilous fight,
O'er the ramparts we watched, were so gallantly streaming?
And the rocket's red glare, the bombs bursting in air,
Gave proof through the night, that our flag was still there.
Oh, say does that Star–Spangled Banner yet wave
O'er the land of the free, and the home of the brave?

On the shore dimly seen, through the mists of the deep,
Where the foe's haughty host, in dread silence reposes,
What is that which the breeze, o'er the towering steep,
As it fitfully blows, half conceals half discloses?
Now it catches the gleam, of the morning's first beam,
In full glory reflected, now shines in the stream:
'Tis the Star–Spangled Banner. Oh long may it wave
O'er the land of the free, and the home of the brave.

And where is that band, who so vauntingly swore
That the havoc of war, and the battle's confusion,
A home and a country, should leave us no more.
Their blood has washed out, their foul footsteps' pollution.
No refuge could save, the hireling and slave
From the terror of flight, or the gloom of the grave:
And the Star–Spangled Banner in triumph doth wave
O'er the land of the free, and the home of the brave.

Oh. thus be it ever, when freemen shall stand
Between their loved home, and the war's desolation.
Blest with victory and peace, may the heav'n rescued land
Praise the Power that hath made, and preserved us a nation.
Then conquer we must, when our cause it is just,
And this be our motto: 'In God is our Trust.'
And the Star–Spangled Banner in triumph shall wave
O'er the land of the free, and the home of the brave.

America the Beautiful

Words by Katharine Lee Bates,
Melody by Samuel Ward

O beautiful for spacious skies, for amber waves of grain,
For purple mountain majesties, above the fruited plain.
America. America. God shed his grace on thee
And crown thy good with brotherhood, From sea to shining sea.

O beautiful for pilgrim feet, whose stern impassioned stress
A thoroughfare of freedom beat, across the wilderness.
America. America. God mend thine every flaw,
Confirm thy soul in self–control, thy liberty in law.

O beautiful for heroes proved, in liberating strife.
Who more than self their country loved, and mercy more than life.
America. America. May God thy gold refine
Till all success be nobleness, and every gain divine.

O beautiful for patriot dream, that sees beyond the years
Thine alabaster cities gleam, undimmed by human tears.
America. America. God shed his grace on thee
And crown thy good with brotherhood, from sea to shining sea.

O beautiful for halcyon skies, for amber waves of grain,
For purple mountain majesties, above the enameled plain.
America. America. God shed his grace on thee
Till souls wax fair as earth and air, and music–hearted sea.

O beautiful for pilgrim's feet, whose stem impassioned stress
A thoroughfare for freedom beat, across the wilderness.
America. America. God shed his grace on thee
Till paths be wrought through, wilds of thought
By pilgrim foot and knee.

O beautiful for glory–tale, Of liberating strife
When once and twice, for man's avail
Men lavished precious life.
America. America., God shed his grace on thee
Till selfish gain no longer stain, the banner of the free.

O beautiful for patriot dream, that sees beyond the years
Thine alabaster cities gleam, undimmed by human tears.
America. America. God shed his grace on thee
Till nobler men keep once again, thy whiter jubilee.

My Country, 'Tis of Thee

*Commonly referred to as '**America**'*
By Reverend Samuel F. Smith

My country, 'tis of Thee, sweet Land of Liberty
Of thee I sing;
Land where my fathers died, land of the pilgrims' pride,
From every mountain side, let Freedom ring.

My native country thee, land of the noble free,
Thy name I love;
I love thy rocks and rills, thy woods and templed hills,
My heart with rapture thrills, Like that above.

Let music swell the breeze, and ring from all the trees
Sweet Freedom's song;
Let mortal tongues awake; let all that breathe partake;
Let rocks their silence break, the sound prolong.

Our fathers' God to Thee, author of Liberty,
To thee we sing,
Long may our land be bright, with Freedom's holy light,
Protect us by thy might, great God, our King.

Our glorious Land to–day, 'Neath Education's sway,
Soars upward still.
Its hills of learning fair, whose bounties all may share,
Behold them everywhere, on vale and hill.

Thy safeguard, Liberty, the school shall ever be,
Our Nation's pride.
No tyrant hand shall smite, while with encircling might
All here are taught the Right, with Truth allied.

Beneath Heaven's gracious will, the stars of progress still
Our course do sway;
In unity sublime, to broader heights we climb,
Triumphant over Time, God speeds our way.

Grand birthright of our sires, our altars and our fires
Keep we still pure.
Our starry flag unfurled, the hope of all the world,
In peace and light impearled, God hold secure.

The Battle Hymn of the Republic

By Julia Ward Howe

Mine eyes have seen the glory of the coming of the Lord
He is trampling out the vintage where the grapes of wrath are stored,
He has loosed the fateful lightening of His terrible swift sword
His truth is marching on.

Glory. Glory. Hallelujah. Glory. Glory. Hallelujah.
Glory. Glory. Hallelujah. His truth is marching on.

I have seen Him in the watch–fires of a hundred circling camps
They have builded Him an altar in the evening dews and damps
I can read His righteous sentence by the dim and flaring lamps
His day is marching on.

Glory. Glory. Hallelujah. Glory. Glory. Hallelujah.
Glory. Glory. Hallelujah. His truth is marching on.

I have read a fiery gospel writ in burnish`d rows of steel,
'As ye deal with my contemners, So with you my grace shall deal;'
Let the Hero, born of woman, crush the serpent with his heel
Since God is marching on.

Glory. Glory. Hallelujah. Glory. Glory. Hallelujah.
Glory. Glory. Hallelujah. His truth is marching on.

He has sounded forth the trumpet that shall never call retreat
He is sifting out the hearts of men before His judgment–seat
Oh, be swift, my soul, to answer Him. be jubilant, my feet.
Our God is marching on.

Glory. Glory. Hallelujah. Glory. Glory. Hallelujah.
Glory. Glory. Hallelujah. His truth is marching on.

In the beauty of the lilies Christ was born across the sea,
With a glory in His bosom that transfigures you and me:

As He died to make men holy, let us die to make men free,
While God is marching on.

Glory. Glory. Hallelujah. Glory. Glory. Hallelujah.
Glory. Glory. Hallelujah. His truth is marching on.

God Bless America

By Irving Berlin
(Spoken introduction)
While the storm clouds gather far across the sea,
Let us swear allegiance to a land that's free,
Let us all be grateful for a land so fair,
As we raise our voices in a solemn prayer:

(Sung)
God Bless America
Land that I love
Stand beside her, and guide her
Thru the night with a light from above
From the mountains, to the prairies
To the oceans, white with foam
God bless America
My home sweet home
God bless America
My home sweet home

XV — The Declaration of Independence

IN CONGRESS, July 4, 1776. The unanimous Declaration of the thirteen united States of America,

When in the Course of human events, it becomes necessary for one people to dissolve the political bands which have connected them with another, and to assume among the powers of the earth, the separate and equal station to which the Laws of Nature and of Nature's God entitle them, a decent respect to the opinions of mankind requires that they should declare the causes which impel them to the separation.

We hold these truths to be self–evident, that all men are created equal, that they are endowed by their Creator with certain unalienable Rights, that among these are Life, Liberty and the pursuit of Happiness.—That to secure these rights, Governments are instituted among Men, deriving their just powers from the consent of the governed, —That whenever any Form of Government becomes destructive of these ends, it is the Right of the People to alter or to abolish it, and to institute new Government, laying its foundation on such principles and organizing its powers in such form, as to them shall seem most likely to effect their Safety and Happiness. Prudence, indeed, will dictate that Governments long established should not be changed for light and transient causes; and accordingly all experience hath shewn, that mankind are more disposed to suffer, while evils are sufferable, than to right themselves by abolishing the forms to which they are accustomed. But when a long train of abuses and usurpations, pursuing invariably the same Object evinces a design to reduce them under absolute Despotism, it is their right, it is their duty, to throw off such Government, and to provide new Guards for their future security.—Such has been the patient sufferance of these Colonies; and such is now the necessity which constrains them to alter their former Systems of Government. The history of the present King of Great Britain is a history of repeated injuries and usurpations, all having in direct object the establishment of an absolute Tyranny over these States. To prove this, let Facts be submitted to a candid world.

- He has refused his Assent to Laws, the most wholesome and necessary for the public good.
- He has forbidden his Governors to pass Laws of immediate and pressing importance, unless suspended in their operation till his Assent should be obtained; and when so suspended, he has utterly neglected to attend to them.
- He has refused to pass other Laws for the accommodation of large districts of people, unless those people would relinquish the right of Representation in the Legislature, a right inestimable to them and formidable to tyrants only.
- He has called together legislative bodies at places unusual, uncomfortable, and distant from the depository of their public Records, for the sole purpose of fatiguing them into compliance with his measures.
- He has dissolved Representative Houses repeatedly, for opposing with manly firmness his invasions on the rights of the people.
- He has refused for a long time, after such dissolutions, to cause others to be elected; whereby the Legislative powers, incapable of Annihilation, have returned to the People at large for their exercise; the State remaining in the mean time exposed to all the dangers of invasion from without, and convulsions within.
- He has endeavoured to prevent the population of these States; for that purpose obstructing the Laws for Naturalization of Foreigners; refusing to pass others to encourage their migra-

tions hither, and raising the conditions of new Appropriations of Lands.

- He has obstructed the Administration of Justice, by refusing his Assent to Laws for establishing Judiciary powers.
- He has made Judges dependent on his Will alone, for the tenure of their offices, and the amount and payment of their salaries.
- He has erected a multitude of New Offices, and sent hither swarms of Officers to harrass our people, and eat out their substance.
- He has kept among us, in times of peace, Standing Armies without the Consent of our legislatures.
- He has affected to render the Military independent of and superior to the Civil power.
- He has combined with others to subject us to a jurisdiction foreign to our Constitution, and unacknowledged by our laws; giving his Assent to their Acts of pretended Legislation:
- For Quartering large bodies of armed troops among us:
- For protecting them, by a mock Trial, from punishment for any Murders which they should commit on the Inhabitants of these States:
- For cutting off our Trade with all parts of the world:
- For imposing Taxes on us without our Consent:
- For depriving us in many cases, of the benefits of Trial by Jury:
- For transporting us beyond Seas to be tried for pretended offences
- For abolishing the free System of English Laws in a neighbouring Province, establishing therein an Arbitrary government,

and enlarging its Boundaries so as to render it at once an example and fit instrument for introducing the same absolute rule into these Colonies:

- For taking away our Charters, abolishing our most valuable Laws, and altering fundamentally the Forms of our Governments:
- For suspending our own Legislatures, and declaring themselves invested with power to legislate for us in all cases whatsoever.
- He has abdicated Government here, by declaring us out of his Protection and waging War against us.
- He has plundered our seas, ravaged our Coasts, burnt our towns, and destroyed the lives of our people.
- He is at this time transporting large Armies of foreign Mercenaries to compleat the works of death, desolation and tyranny, already begun with circumstances of Cruelty & perfidy scarcely paralleled in the most barbarous ages, and totally unworthy the Head of a civilized nation.
- He has constrained our fellow Citizens taken Captive on the high Seas to bear Arms against their Country, to become the executioners of their friends and Brethren, or to fall themselves by their Hands.
- He has excited domestic insurrections amongst us, and has endeavoured to bring on the inhabitants of our frontiers, the merciless Indian Savages, whose known rule of warfare, is an undistinguished destruction of all ages, sexes and conditions.

In every stage of these Oppressions We have Petitioned for Redress in the most humble terms: Our repeated Petitions have been answered only by repeated injury. A Prince whose character is thus marked by every act which may define a Tyrant, is unfit to be the ruler of a free people.

Nor have We been wanting in attentions to our Brittish brethren. We have warned them from time to time of attempts by their legislature to extend an unwarrantable jurisdiction over us. We have reminded them of the circumstances of our emigration and settlement here. We have appealed to their native justice and magnanimity, and we have conjured them by the ties of our common kindred to disavow these usurpations, which, would inevitably interrupt our connections and correspondence. They too have been deaf to the voice of justice and of consanguinity. We must, therefore, acquiesce in the necessity, which denounces our Separation, and hold them, as we hold the rest of mankind, Enemies in War, in Peace Friends.

We, therefore, the Representatives of the united States of America, in General Congress, Assembled, appealing to the Supreme Judge of the world for the rectitude of our intentions, do, in the Name, and by Authority of the good People of these Colonies, solemnly publish and declare, That these United Colonies are, and of Right ought to be Free and Independent States; that they are Absolved from all Allegiance to the British Crown, and that all political connection between them and the State of Great Britain, is and ought to be totally dissolved; and that as Free and Independent States, they have full Power to levy War, conclude Peace, contract Alliances, establish Commerce, and to do all other Acts and Things which Independent States may of right do. And for the support of this Declaration, with a firm reliance on the protection of divine Providence, we mutually pledge to each other our Lives, our Fortunes and our sacred Honor.

The 56 signatures on the Declaration appear in the positions indicated:

Georgia:
Button Gwinnett
Lyman Hall
George Walton

North Carolina:
William Hooper
Joseph Hewes
John Penn

South Carolina:
Edward Rutledge
Thomas Heyward, Jr.
Thomas Lynch, Jr.
Arthur Middleton

New York:
William Floyd
Philip Livingston
Francis Lewis
Lewis Morris

Connecticut:
Roger Sherman
Samuel Huntington
William Williams
Oliver Wolcott

New Hampshire:
Matthew Thornton

Massachusetts:
John Hancock

Maryland:
Samuel Chase
William Paca
Thomas Stone
Charles Carroll of Carrollton

Virginia:
George Wythe
Richard Henry Lee
Thomas Jefferson
Benjamin Harrison
Thomas Nelson, Jr.
Francis Lightfoot Lee
Carter Braxton

Pennsylvania:
Robert Morris
Benjamin Rush
Benjamin Franklin
John Morton
George Clymer
James Smith
George Taylor
James Wilson
George Ross

Delaware:
Caesar Rodney
George Read
Thomas McKean

New Jersey:
Richard Stockton
John Witherspoon
Francis Hopkinson
John Hart
Abraham Clark

New Hampshire:
Josiah Bartlett
William Whipple

Massachusetts:
Samuel Adams
John Adams
Robert Treat Paine
Elbridge Gerry

Rhode Island:
Stephen Hopkins
William Ellery

XVI — The Bill of Rights, Amendments 1–10

The Preamble to The Bill of Rights

Congress of the United States begun and held at the City of New–York, on Wednesday the fourth of March, one thousand seven hundred and eighty nine.

THE Conventions of a number of the States, having at the time of their adopting the Constitution, expressed a desire, in order to prevent misconstruction or abuse of its powers, that further declaratory and restrictive clauses should be added: And as extending the ground of public confidence in the Government, will best ensure the beneficent ends of its institution.

RESOLVED by the Senate and House of Representatives of the United States of America, in Congress assembled, two thirds of both Houses concurring, that the following Articles be proposed to the Legislatures of the several States, as amendments to the Constitution of the United States, all, or any of which Articles, when ratified by three fourths of the said Legislatures, to be valid to all intents and purposes, as part of the said Constitution; viz.

ARTICLES in addition to, and Amendment of the Constitution of the United States of America, proposed by Congress, and ratified by the Legislatures of the several States, pursuant to the fifth Article of the original Constitution.

Congress of the United States begun and held at the City of New–York, on Wednesday the fourth of March, one thousand seven hundred and eighty nine.

THE Conventions of a number of the States, having at the time of their adopting the Constitution, expressed a desire, in order to prevent misconstruction or abuse of its powers, that further declaratory and restrictive clauses should be added: And as extending the ground of public confidence in the Government, will best ensure the beneficent ends of its institution.

RESOLVED by the Senate and House of Representatives of the United States of America, in Congress assembled, two thirds of both Houses concurring, that the following Articles be proposed to the Legislatures of the several States, as amendments to the Constitution of the United States, all, or any of which Articles, when ratified by three fourths of the said Legislatures, to be valid to all intents and purposes, as part of the said Constitution; viz.

ARTICLES in addition to, and Amendment of the Constitution of the United States of America, proposed by Congress, and ratified by the Legislatures of the several States, pursuant to the fifth Article of the original Constitution.

Note: The following text is a transcription of the first ten amendments to the Constitution in their original form. These amendments were ratified December 15, 1791, and form what is known as the 'Bill of Rights.'

Amendment I

Congress shall make no law respecting an establishment of religion, or prohibiting the free exercise thereof; or abridging the freedom of speech, or of the press; or the right of the people peaceably to assemble, and to petition the Government for a redress of grievances.

Amendment II

A well regulated Militia, being necessary to the security of a free State, the right of the people to keep and bear Arms, shall not be infringed.

Amendment III

No Soldier shall, in time of peace be quartered in any house, without the consent of the Owner, nor in time of war, but in a manner to be prescribed by law.

Amendment IV

The right of the people to be secure in their persons, houses, papers, and effects, against unreasonable searches and seizures, shall not be violated, and no Warrants shall issue, but upon probable cause, supported by Oath or affirmation, and particularly describing the place to be searched, and the persons or things to be seized.

Amendment V

No person shall be held to answer for a capital, or otherwise infamous crime, unless on a presentment or indictment of a Grand Jury, except in cases arising in the land or naval forces, or in the Militia, when in actual service in time of War or public danger; nor shall any person be subject for the same offence to be twice put in jeopardy of life or limb; nor shall be compelled in any criminal case to be a witness against himself, nor be deprived of life, liberty, or property, without due process of law; nor shall private property be taken for public use, without just compensation.

Amendment VI

In all criminal prosecutions, the accused shall enjoy the right to a speedy and public trial, by an impartial jury of the State and district wherein the crime shall have been committed, which district shall have been previously ascertained by law, and to be informed of the nature and cause of the accusation; to be confronted with the witnesses against him; to have compulsory process for obtaining witnesses in his favor, and to have the Assistance of Counsel for his defence.

Amendment VII

In Suits at common law, where the value in controversy shall exceed twenty dollars, the right of trial by jury shall be preserved, and no fact tried by a jury, shall be otherwise re–examined in any Court of the United States, than according to the rules of the common law.

Amendment VIII

Excessive bail shall not be required, nor excessive fines imposed, nor cruel and unusual punishments inflicted.

Amendment IX

The enumeration in the Constitution, of certain rights, shall not be construed to deny or disparage others retained by the people.

Amendment X

The powers not delegated to the United States by the Constitution, nor prohibited by it to the States, are reserved to the States respectively, or to the people.

XVII — The Constitution of the United States, Amendments 11–27

Amendment XI

Passed by Congress March 4, 1794. Ratified February 7, 1795.

Note: Article III, section 2, of the Constitution was modified by amendment 11.

The Judicial power of the United States shall not be construed to extend to any suit in law or equity, commenced or prosecuted against one of the United States by Citizens of another State, or by Citizens or Subjects of any Foreign State.

Amendment XII

Passed by Congress December 9, 1803. Ratified June 15, 1804.

Note: A portion of Article II, section 1 of the Constitution was superseded by the 12th amendment.

The Electors shall meet in their respective states and vote by ballot for President and Vice–President, one of whom, at least, shall not be an inhabitant of the same state with themselves; they shall name in their ballots the person voted for as President, and in distinct ballots the person voted for as Vice–President, and they shall make distinct lists of all persons voted for as President, and of all persons voted for as Vice–President, and of the number of votes for each, which lists they shall sign and certify, and transmit sealed to the seat of the government of the United States, directed to the President of the Senate; — the President of the Senate shall, in the presence of the Senate and House of Representatives, open all the certificates and the votes shall then be counted; — The person having the greatest number of votes for President, shall be the President, if such number be a majority of the whole number of Electors appointed; and if no person have such majority, then from the persons having the highest numbers not exceeding three on the list of those voted for as President, the House of Representatives shall choose immediately, by ballot, the President. But in choosing the President, the votes shall be taken by states, the representation from each state having one vote; a quorum for this purpose shall consist of a member or members from two–thirds of the states, and a majority of all the states shall be necessary to a choice. [And if the House of Representatives shall not choose a President whenever the right of choice shall devolve upon them, before the fourth day of March next following, then the Vice–President shall act as President, as in case of the death or other Constitutional disability of the President. —]* The person having the greatest number of votes as Vice–President, shall be the Vice–President, if such number be a majority of the whole number of Electors appointed, and if no person have a majority, then from the two highest numbers on the list, the Senate shall choose the Vice–President; a quorum for the purpose shall consist of two–thirds of the whole number of Senators, and a majority of the whole number shall be necessary to a choice. But no person Constitutionally ineligible to the office of President shall be eligible to that of Vice–President of the United States.

*Superseded by section 3 of the 20th amendment.

Amendment XIII

Passed by Congress January 31, 1865. Ratified December 6, 1865.

Note: A portion of Article IV, section 2, of the Constitution was superseded by the 13th amendment.

Section 1: Neither slavery nor involuntary servitude, except as a punishment for crime whereof the party shall have been duly convicted, shall exist within the United States, or any place subject to their jurisdiction.

Section 2: Congress shall have power to enforce this article by appropriate legislation.

Amendment XIV

Passed by Congress June 13, 1866. Ratified July 9, 1868.

Note: Article I, section 2, of the Constitution was modified by section 2 of the 14th amendment.

Section 1: All persons born or naturalized in the United States, and subject to the jurisdiction thereof, are citizens of the United States and of the State wherein they reside. No State shall make or enforce any law which shall abridge the privileges or immunities of citizens of the United States; nor shall any State deprive any person of life, liberty, or property, without due process of law; nor deny to any person within its jurisdiction the equal protection of the laws.

Section 2: Representatives shall be apportioned among the several States according to their respective numbers, counting the whole number of persons in each State, excluding Indians not taxed. But when the right to vote at any election for the choice of electors for President and Vice–President of the United States, Representatives in Congress, the Executive and Judicial officers of a State, or the members of the Legislature thereof, is denied to any of the male inhabitants of such State, being twenty–one years of age,* and citizens of the United States, or in any way abridged, except for participation in rebellion, or other crime, the basis of representation therein shall be reduced in the proportion which the number of such male citizens shall bear to the whole number of male citizens twenty–one years of age in such State.

Section 3: No person shall be a Senator or Representative in Congress, or elector of President and Vice–President, or hold any office, civil or military, under the United States, or under any State, who, having previously taken an oath, as a member of Congress, or as an officer of the United States, or as a member of any State legislature, or as an executive or judicial officer of any State, to support the Constitution of the United States, shall have engaged in insurrection or rebellion against the same, or given aid or comfort to the enemies thereof. But Congress may by a vote of two–thirds of each House, remove such disability.

Section 4: The validity of the public debt of the United States, authorized by law, including debts incurred for payment of pensions and bounties for services in suppressing insurrection or rebellion, shall not be questioned. But neither the United States nor any State shall assume or pay any debt or obligation incurred in aid of insurrection or rebellion against the United States, or any claim for the loss or emancipation of any slave; but all such debts, obligations and claims shall be held illegal and void.

Section 5: The Congress shall have the power to enforce, by appropriate legislation, the provisions of this article.

*Changed by section 1 of the 26th amendment.

Amendment XV

Passed by Congress February 26, 1869. Ratified February 3, 1870.

Section 1: The right of citizens of the United States to vote shall not be denied or abridged by the United States or by any State on account of race, color, or previous condition of servitude—

Section 2: The Congress shall have the power to enforce this article by appropriate legislation.

Amendment XVI

Passed by Congress July 2, 1909. Ratified February 3, 1913.

Note: Article I, section 9, of the Constitution was modified by amendment 16.

The Congress shall have power to lay and collect taxes on incomes, from whatever source derived, without apportionment among the several States, and without regard to any census or enumeration.

Amendment XVII

Passed by Congress May 13, 1912. Ratified April 8, 1913.

Note: Article I, section 3, of the Constitution was modified by the 17th amendment.

The Senate of the United States shall be composed of two Senators from each State, elected by the people thereof, for six years; and each Senator shall have one vote. The electors in each State shall have the qualifications requisite for electors of the most numerous branch of the State legislatures.

When vacancies happen in the representation of any State in the Senate, the executive authority of such State shall issue writs of election to fill such vacancies: Provided, That the legislature of any State may empower the executive thereof to make temporary appointments until the people fill the vacancies by election as the legislature may direct.

This amendment shall not be so construed as to affect the election or term of any Senator chosen before it becomes valid as part of the Constitution.

Amendment XVIII

Passed by Congress December 18, 1917. Ratified January 16, 1919. Repealed by amendment 21.

Section 1: After one year from the ratification of this article the manufacture, sale, or transportation of intoxicating liquors within, the importation thereof into, or the exportation thereof from the United States and all territory subject to the jurisdiction thereof for beverage purposes is hereby prohibited.

Section 2: The Congress and the several States shall have concurrent power to enforce this article by appropriate legislation.

Section 3: This article shall be inoperative unless it shall have been ratified as an amendment to the Constitution by the legislatures of the several States, as provided in the Constitution, within seven years from the date of the submission hereof to the States by the Congress.

Amendment XIX

Passed by Congress June 4, 1919. Ratified August 18, 1920.

The right of citizens of the United States to vote shall not be denied or abridged by the United States or by any State on account of sex.

Congress shall have power to enforce this article by appropriate legislation.

Amendment XX

Passed by Congress March 2, 1932. Ratified January 23, 1933.

Note: Article I, section 4, of the Constitution was modified by section 2 of this amendment. In addition, a portion of the 12th amendment was superseded by section 3.

Section 1: The terms of the President and the Vice President shall end at noon on the 20th day of January, and the terms of Senators and Representatives at noon on the 3d day of January, of the years in which such terms would have ended if this article had not been ratified; and the terms of their successors shall then begin.

Section 2: The Congress shall assemble at least once in every year, and such meeting shall begin at noon on the 3d day of January, unless they shall by law appoint a different day.

Section 3: If, at the time fixed for the beginning of the term of the President, the President elect shall have died, the Vice President elect shall become President. If a President shall not have been chosen before the time fixed for the beginning of his term, or if the President elect shall have failed to qualify, then the Vice President elect shall act as President until a President shall have qualified; and the Congress may by law provide for the case wherein neither a President elect nor a Vice President shall have qualified, declaring who shall then act as President, or the manner in which one who is to act shall be selected, and such person shall act accordingly until a President or Vice President shall have qualified.

Section 4: The Congress may by law provide for the case of the death of any of the persons from whom the House of Representatives may choose a President whenever the right of choice shall have devolved upon them, and for the case of the death of any of the persons from whom the Senate may choose a Vice President whenever the right of choice shall have devolved upon them.

Section 5: Sections 1 and 2 shall take effect on the 15th day of October following the ratification of this article.

Section 6: This article shall be inoperative unless it shall have been ratified as an amendment to the Constitution by the legislatures of three–fourths of the several States within seven years from the date of its submission.

Amendment XXI

Passed by Congress February 20, 1933. Ratified December 5, 1933.

Section 1: The eighteenth article of amendment to the Constitution of the United States is hereby repealed.

Section 2: The transportation or importation into any State, Territory, or Possession of the United States for delivery or use therein of intoxicating liquors, in violation of the laws thereof, is hereby prohibited.

Section 3: This article shall be inoperative unless it shall have been ratified as an amendment to the Constitution by conventions in the several States, as provided in the Constitution, within seven years from the date of the submission hereof to the States by the Congress.

Amendment XXII

Passed by Congress March 21, 1947. Ratified February 27, 1951.

Section 1: No person shall be elected to the office of the President more than twice, and no person who has held the office of President, or acted as President, for more than two years of a term to which some other person was elected President shall be elected to the office of President more than once. But this Article shall not apply to any person holding the office of President when this Article was proposed by Congress, and shall not prevent any person who may be holding the office of President, or acting as President, during the term within which this Article becomes operative from holding the office of President or acting as President during the remainder of such term.

Section 2: This article shall be inoperative unless it shall have been ratified as an amendment to the Constitution by the legislatures of three–fourths of the several States within seven years from the date of its submission to the States by the Congress.

Amendment XXIII

Passed by Congress June 16, 1960. Ratified March 29, 1961.

Section 1: The District constituting the seat of Government of the United States shall appoint in such manner as Congress may direct:

A number of electors of President and Vice President equal to the whole number of Senators and Representatives in Congress to which the District would be entitled if it were a State, but in no event more than the least populous State; they shall be in addition to those appointed by the States, but they shall be considered, for the purposes of the election of President and Vice President, to be electors appointed by a State; and they shall meet in the District and perform such duties as provided by the twelfth article of amendment.

Section 2: The Congress shall have power to enforce this article by appropriate legislation.

Amendment XXIV

Passed by Congress August 27, 1962. Ratified January 23, 1964.

Section 1: The right of citizens of the United States to vote in any primary or other election for President or Vice President, for electors for President or Vice President, or for Senator or Representative in Congress, shall not be denied or abridged by the United States or any State by reason of failure to pay poll tax or other tax.

Section 2: The Congress shall have power to enforce this article by appropriate legislation.

Amendment XXV

Passed by Congress July 6, 1965. Ratified February 10, 1967.

Note: Article II, section 1, of the Constitution was affected by the 25th amendment.

Section 1: In case of the removal of the President from office or of his death or resignation, the Vice President shall become President.

Section 2: Whenever there is a vacancy in the office of the Vice President, the President shall nominate a Vice President who shall take office upon confirmation by a majority vote of both Houses of Congress.

Section 3: Whenever the President transmits to the President pro tempore of the Senate and the Speaker of the House of Representatives his written declaration that he is unable to discharge the powers and duties of his office, and until he transmits to them a written declaration to the contrary, such powers and duties shall be discharged by the Vice President as Acting President.

Section 4: Whenever the Vice President and a majority of either the principal officers of the executive departments or of such other body as Congress may by law provide, transmit to the President pro tempore of the Senate and the Speaker of the House of Representatives their written declaration that the President is unable to discharge the powers and duties of his office, the Vice President shall immediately assume the powers and duties of the office as Acting President.

Thereafter, when the President transmits to the President pro tempore of the Senate and the Speaker of the House of Representatives his written declaration that no inability exists, he shall resume the powers and duties of his office unless the Vice President and a majority of either the principal officers of the executive department or of such other body as Congress may by law provide, transmit within four days to the President pro tempore of the Senate and the Speaker of the House of Representatives their written declaration that the President is unable to discharge the powers and duties of his office. Thereupon Congress shall decide the issue, assembling within forty–eight hours for that purpose if not in session. If the Congress, within twenty–one days after receipt of the latter written declaration, or, if Congress is not in session, within twenty–one days after Congress is required to assemble, determines by two–thirds vote of both Houses that the President is unable to discharge the powers and duties of his office, the Vice President shall continue to discharge the same as Acting President; otherwise, the President shall resume the powers and duties of his office.

Amendment XXVI

Passed by Congress March 23, 1971. Ratified July 1, 1971.

Note: Amendment 14, section 2, of the Constitution was modified by section 1 of the 26th amendment.

Section 1: The right of citizens of the United States, who are eighteen years of age or older, to vote shall not be denied or abridged by the United States or by any State on account of age.

Section 2: The Congress shall have power to enforce this article by appropriate legislation.

Amendment XXVII

Originally proposed Sept. 25, 1789. Ratified May 7, 1992.

No law, varying the compensation for the services of the Senators and Representatives, shall take effect, until an election of representatives shall have intervened.

XVIII — The Constitution of the United States

We the People of the United States, in Order to form a more perfect Union, establish Justice, insure domestic Tranquility, provide for the common defence, promote the general Welfare, and secure the Blessings of Liberty to ourselves and our Posterity, do ordain and establish this Constitution for the United States of America.

Article I

Section 1: All legislative Powers herein granted shall be vested in a Congress of the United States, which shall consist of a Senate and House of Representatives.

Section 2: The House of Representatives shall be composed of Members chosen every second Year by the People of the several States, and the Electors in each State shall have the Qualifications requisite for Electors of the most numerous Branch of the State Legislature.

No Person shall be a Representative who shall not have attained to the Age of twenty five Years, and been seven Years a Citizen of the United States, and who shall not, when elected, be an Inhabitant of that State in which he shall be chosen.

Representatives and direct Taxes shall be apportioned among the several States which may be included within this Union, according to their respective Numbers, which shall be determined by adding to the whole Number of free Persons, including those bound to Service for a Term of Years, and excluding Indians not taxed, three fifths of all other Persons. The actual Enumeration shall be made within three Years after the first Meeting of the Congress of the United States, and within every subsequent Term of ten Years, in such Manner as they shall by Law direct. The Number of Representatives shall not exceed one for every thirty Thousand, but each State shall have at Least one

Representative; and until such enumeration shall be made, the State of New Hampshire shall be entitled to chuse three, Massachusetts eight, Rhode–Island and Providence Plantations one, Connecticut five, New–York six, New Jersey four, Pennsylvania eight, Delaware one, Maryland six, Virginia ten, North Carolina five, South Carolina five, and Georgia three.

When vacancies happen in the Representation from any State, the Executive Authority thereof shall issue Writs of Election to fill such Vacancies.

The House of Representatives shall chuse their Speaker and other Officers; and shall have the sole Power of Impeachment.

Section 3: The Senate of the United States shall be composed of two Senators from each State, chosen by the Legislature thereof for six Years; and each Senator shall have one Vote.

Immediately after they shall be assembled in Consequence of the first Election, they shall be divided as equally as may be into three Classes. The Seats of the Senators of the first Class shall be vacated at the Expiration of the second Year, of the second Class at the Expiration of the fourth Year, and of the third Class at the Expiration of the sixth Year, so that one third may be chosen every second Year; and if Vacancies happen by Resignation, or otherwise, during the Recess of the Legislature of any State, the Executive thereof may make temporary Appointments until the next Meeting of the Legislature, which shall then fill such Vacancies.

No Person shall be a Senator who shall not have attained to the Age of thirty Years, and been nine Years a Citizen of the United States, and who shall not, when elected, be an Inhabitant of that State for which he shall be chosen.

The Vice President of the United States shall be President of the Senate, but shall have no Vote, unless they be equally divided.

The Senate shall chuse their other Officers, and also a President pro tempore, in the Absence of the Vice President, or when he shall exercise the Office of President of the United States.

The Senate shall have the sole Power to try all Impeachments. When sitting for that Purpose, they shall be on Oath or Affirmation. When the President of the United States is tried, the Chief Justice shall preside: And no Person shall be convicted without the Concurrence of two thirds of the Members present.

Judgment in Cases of Impeachment shall not extend further than to removal from Office, and disqualification to hold and enjoy any Office of honor, Trust or Profit under the United States: but the Party convicted shall nevertheless be liable and subject to Indictment, Trial, Judgment and Punishment, according to Law.

Section 4: The Times, Places and Manner of holding Elections for Senators and Representatives, shall be prescribed in each State by the Legislature thereof; but the Congress may at any time by Law make or alter such Regulations, except as to the Places of chusing Senators.

The Congress shall assemble at least once in every Year, and such Meeting shall be on the first Monday in December, unless they shall by Law appoint a different Day.

Section 5: Each House shall be the Judge of the Elections, Returns and Qualifications of its own Members, and a Majority of each shall constitute a Quorum to do Business; but a smaller Number may adjourn from day to day, and may be authorized to compel the Attendance of absent Members, in such Manner, and under such Penalties as each House may provide.

Each House may determine the Rules of its Proceedings, punish its Members for disorderly Behaviour, and, with the Concurrence of two thirds, expel a Member.

Each House shall keep a Journal of its Proceedings, and from time to time publish the same, excepting such Parts as may in their Judgment require Secrecy; and the Yeas and Nays of the Members of either House on any question shall, at the Desire of one fifth of those Present, be entered on the Journal.

Neither House, during the Session of Congress, shall, without the Consent of the other, adjourn for more than three days, nor to any other Place than that in which the two Houses shall be sitting.

Section 6: The Senators and Representatives shall receive a Compensation for their Services, to be ascertained by Law, and paid out of the Treasury of the United States. They shall in all Cases, except Treason, Felony and Breach of the Peace, be privileged from Arrest during their Attendance at the Session of their respective Houses, and in going to and returning from the same; and for any Speech or Debate in either House, they shall not be questioned in any other Place.

No Senator or Representative shall, during the Time for which he was elected, be appointed to any civil Office under the Authority of the United States, which shall have been created, or the Emoluments whereof shall have been encreased during such time; and no Person holding any Office under the United States, shall be a Member of either House during his Continuance in Office.

Section 7: All Bills for raising Revenue shall originate in the House of Representatives; but the Senate may propose or concur with Amendments as on other Bills.

Every Bill which shall have passed the House of Representatives and the Senate, shall, before it become a Law, be presented to the President of the United States: If he approve he shall sign it, but if not he shall return it, with his Objections to that House in which it shall have originated, who shall enter the Objections at large on their Journal, and proceed to reconsider it. If after such Reconsideration two thirds of that House shall agree to pass the Bill, it shall be sent, together with the Objections, to the other House, by which it shall likewise be reconsidered, and if approved by two thirds of that House, it shall become a Law. But in all such Cases the Votes of both Houses shall be determined by yeas and Nays, and the Names of the Persons voting for and against the Bill shall be entered on the Journal of each House respectively. If any Bill shall not be returned by the President within ten Days (Sundays excepted) after it shall have been presented to him, the Same shall be a Law, in like Manner as if he had signed it, unless the Congress by their Adjournment prevent its Return, in which Case it shall not be a Law.

Every Order, Resolution, or Vote to which the Concurrence of the Senate and House of Representatives may be necessary (except on a question of Adjournment) shall be presented to the President of the United States; and before the Same shall take Effect, shall be approved by him, or being disapproved by him, shall be repassed by two thirds of the Senate and House of Representatives, according to the Rules and Limitations prescribed in the Case of a Bill.

Section 8: The Congress shall have Power To lay and collect Taxes, Duties, Imposts and Excises, to pay the Debts and provide for the common Defence and general Welfare of the United States; but all Duties, Imposts and Excises shall be uniform throughout the United States;

To borrow Money on the credit of the United States;

To regulate Commerce with foreign Nations, and among the several States, and with the Indian Tribes;

To establish an uniform Rule of Naturalization, and uniform Laws on the subject of Bankruptcies throughout the United States;

To coin Money, regulate the Value thereof, and of foreign Coin, and fix the Standard of Weights and Measures;

To provide for the Punishment of counterfeiting the Securities and current Coin of the United States;

To establish Post Offices and post Roads;

To promote the Progress of Science and useful Arts, by securing for limited Times to Authors and Inventors the exclusive Right to their respective Writings and Discoveries;

To constitute Tribunals inferior to the supreme Court;

To define and punish Piracies and Felonies committed on the high Seas, and Offences against the Law of Nations;

To declare War, grant Letters of Marque and Reprisal, and make Rules concerning Captures on Land and Water;

To raise and support Armies, but no Appropriation of Money to that Use shall be for a longer Term than two Years;

To provide and maintain a Navy;

To make Rules for the Government and Regulation of the land and naval Forces;

To provide for calling forth the Militia to execute the Laws of the Union, suppress Insurrections and repel Invasions;

To provide for organizing, arming, and disciplining, the Militia, and for governing such Part of them as may be employed in the Service of the United States, reserving to the States respectively, the Appointment of the Officers, and the Authority of training the Militia according to the discipline prescribed by Congress;

To exercise exclusive Legislation in all Cases whatsoever, over such District (not exceeding ten Miles square) as may, by Cession of particular States, and the Acceptance of Congress, become the Seat of the Government of the United States, and to exercise like Authority over all Places purchased by the Consent of the Legislature of the State in which the Same shall be, for the Erection of Forts, Magazines, Arsenals, dock–Yards, and other needful Buildings;—And

To make all Laws which shall be necessary and proper for carrying into Execution the foregoing Powers, and all other Powers vested by this Constitution in the Government of the United States, or in any Department or Officer thereof.

Section 9: The Migration or Importation of such Persons as any of the States now existing shall think proper to admit, shall not be prohibited by the Congress prior to the Year one thousand eight hundred and eight, but a Tax or duty may be imposed on such Importation, not exceeding ten dollars for each Person.

The Privilege of the Writ of Habeas Corpus shall not be suspended, unless when in Cases of Rebellion or Invasion the public Safety may require it.

No Bill of Attainder or ex post facto Law shall be passed.

No Capitation, or other direct, Tax shall be laid, unless in Proportion to the Census or enumeration herein before directed to be taken.

No Tax or Duty shall be laid on Articles exported from any State.

No Preference shall be given by any Regulation of Commerce or Revenue to the Ports of one State over those of another; nor shall Vessels bound to, or from, one State, be obliged to enter, clear, or pay Duties in another.

No Money shall be drawn from the Treasury, but in Consequence of Appropriations made by Law; and a regular Statement and Account of the Receipts and Expenditures of all public Money shall be published from time to time.

No Title of Nobility shall be granted by the United States: And no Person holding any Office of Profit or Trust under them, shall, without the Consent of the Congress, accept of any present, Emolument, Office, or Title, of any kind whatever, from any King, Prince, or foreign State.

Section 10: No State shall enter into any Treaty, Alliance, or Confederation; grant Letters of Marque and Reprisal; coin Money; emit Bills of Credit; make any Thing but gold and silver Coin a Tender in Payment of Debts; pass any Bill of Attainder, ex post facto Law, or Law impairing the Obligation of Contracts, or grant any Title of Nobility.

No State shall, without the Consent of the Congress, lay any Imposts or Duties on Imports or Exports, except what may be absolutely necessary for executing it's inspection Laws: and the net Produce of all Duties and Imposts, laid by any State on Imports or Exports, shall be for the Use of the Treasury of the United States; and all such Laws shall be subject to the Revision and Controul of the Congress.

No State shall, without the Consent of Congress, lay any Duty of Tonnage, keep Troops, or Ships of War in time of Peace, enter into any Agreement or Compact with another State, or with a foreign Power, or engage in War, unless actually invaded, or in such imminent Danger as will not admit of delay.

Article II

Section 1: The executive Power shall be vested in a President of the United States of America. He shall hold his Office during the Term of four Years, and, together with the Vice President, chosen for the same Term, be elected, as follows:

Each State shall appoint, in such Manner as the Legislature thereof may direct, a Number of Electors, equal to the whole Number of Senators and Representatives to which the State may be entitled in the Congress: but no Senator or Representative, or Person holding an Office of Trust or Profit under the United States, shall be appointed an Elector.

The Electors shall meet in their respective States, and vote by Ballot for two Persons, of whom one at least shall not be an Inhabitant of the same State with themselves. And they shall make a List of all the Persons voted for, and of the Number of Votes for each; which List they shall sign and certify, and transmit sealed to the Seat of the Government of the United States, directed to the President of the Senate. The President of the Senate shall, in the Presence of the Senate and House of Representatives, open all the Certificates, and the Votes shall then be counted. The Person having the greatest Number of Votes shall be the President, if such Number be a Majority of the whole Number of Electors appointed; and if there be more than one who have such Majority, and have an equal Number of Votes, then the House of Representatives shall immediately chuse by Ballot one of them for President; and if no Person have a Majority, then from the five highest on the List the said House shall in like Manner chuse the President. But in chusing the President, the Votes shall be taken by States, the Representation from each State having one Vote; A quorum for this purpose shall consist of a Member or Members from two thirds of the States, and a Majority of all the States shall be necessary to a Choice. In every

Case, after the Choice of the President, the Person having the greatest Number of Votes of the Electors shall be the Vice President. But if there should remain two or more who have equal Votes, the Senate shall chuse from them by Ballot the Vice President.

The Congress may determine the Time of chusing the Electors, and the Day on which they shall give their Votes; which Day shall be the same throughout the United States.

No Person except a natural born Citizen, or a Citizen of the United States, at the time of the Adoption of this Constitution, shall be eligible to the Office of President; neither shall any Person be eligible to that Office who shall not have attained to the Age of thirty five Years, and been fourteen Years a Resident within the United States.

In Case of the Removal of the President from Office, or of his Death, Resignation, or Inability to discharge the Powers and Duties of the said Office, the Same shall devolve on the Vice President, and the Congress may by Law provide for the Case of Removal, Death, Resignation or Inability, both of the President and Vice President, declaring what Officer shall then act as President, and such Officer shall act accordingly, until the Disability be removed, or a President shall be elected.

The President shall, at stated Times, receive for his Services, a Compensation, which shall neither be increased nor diminished during the Period for which he shall have been elected, and he shall not receive within that Period any other Emolument from the United States, or any of them.

Before he enter on the Execution of his Office, he shall take the following Oath or Affirmation:—'I do solemnly swear (or affirm) that I will faithfully execute the Office of President of the

United States, and will to the best of my Ability, preserve, protect and defend the Constitution of the United States.'

Section 2: The President shall be Commander in Chief of the Army and Navy of the United States, and of the Militia of the several States, when called into the actual Service of the United States; he may require the Opinion, in writing, of the principal Officer in each of the executive Departments, upon any Subject relating to the Duties of their respective Offices, and he shall have Power to grant Reprieves and Pardons for Offences against the United States, except in Cases of Impeachment.

He shall have Power, by and with the Advice and Consent of the Senate, to make Treaties, provided two thirds of the Senators present concur; and he shall nominate, and by and with the Advice and Consent of the Senate, shall appoint Ambassadors, other public Ministers and Consuls, Judges of the supreme Court, and all other Officers of the United States, whose Appointments are not herein otherwise provided for, and which shall be established by Law: but the Congress may by Law vest the Appointment of such inferior Officers, as they think proper, in the President alone, in the Courts of Law, or in the Heads of Departments.

The President shall have Power to fill up all Vacancies that may happen during the Recess of the Senate, by granting Commissions which shall expire at the End of their next Session.

Section 3: He shall from time to time give to the Congress Information of the State of the Union, and recommend to their Consideration such Measures as he shall judge necessary and expedient; he may, on extraordinary Occasions, convene both Houses, or either of them, and in Case of Disagreement between them, with Respect to the Time of Adjournment, he may adjourn them to such Time as he shall think proper; he shall receive Ambassadors and other public Ministers; he shall take Care that the Laws be faithfully executed, and shall Commission all the Officers of the United States.

Section 4: The President, Vice President and all civil Officers of the United States, shall be removed from Office on Impeachment for, and Conviction of, Treason, Bribery, or other high Crimes and Misdemeanors.

Article III

Section 1: The judicial Power of the United States shall be vested in one supreme Court, and in such inferior Courts as the Congress may from time to time ordain and establish. The Judges, both of the supreme and inferior Courts, shall hold their Offices during good Behaviour, and shall, at stated Times, receive for their Services a Compensation, which shall not be diminished during their Continuance in Office.

Section 2: The judicial Power shall extend to all Cases, in Law and Equity, arising under this Constitution, the Laws of the United States, and Treaties made, or which shall be made, under their Authority;—to all Cases affecting Ambassadors, other public Ministers and Consuls;—to all Cases of admiralty and maritime Jurisdiction;—to Controversies to which the United States shall be a Party;—to Controversies between two or more States;— between a State and Citizens of another State,—between Citizens of different States,—between Citizens of the same State claiming Lands under Grants of different States, and between a State, or the Citizens thereof, and foreign States, Citizens or Subjects.

In all Cases affecting Ambassadors, other public Ministers and Consuls, and those in which a State shall be Party, the supreme Court shall have original Jurisdiction. In all the other Cases before mentioned, the supreme Court shall have appellate

Jurisdiction, both as to Law and Fact, with such Exceptions, and under such Regulations as the Congress shall make.

The Trial of all Crimes, except in Cases of Impeachment, shall be by Jury; and such Trial shall be held in the State where the said Crimes shall have been committed; but when not committed within any State, the Trial shall be at such Place or Places as the Congress may by Law have directed.

Section 3: Treason against the United States, shall consist only in levying War against them, or in adhering to their Enemies, giving them Aid and Comfort. No Person shall be convicted of Treason unless on the Testimony of two Witnesses to the same overt Act, or on Confession in open Court.

The Congress shall have Power to declare the Punishment of Treason, but no Attainder of Treason shall work Corruption of Blood, or Forfeiture except during the Life of the Person attainted.

Article IV

Section 1: Full Faith and Credit shall be given in each State to the public Acts, Records, and judicial Proceedings of every other State. And the Congress may by general Laws prescribe the Manner in which such Acts, Records and Proceedings shall be proved, and the Effect thereof.

Section 2: The Citizens of each State shall be entitled to all Privileges and Immunities of Citizens in the several States.

A Person charged in any State with Treason, Felony, or other Crime, who shall flee from Justice, and be found in another State, shall on Demand of the executive Authority of the State from which he fled, be delivered up, to be removed to the State having Jurisdiction of the Crime.

No Person held to Service or Labour in one State, under the Laws thereof, escaping into another, shall, in Consequence of any Law or Regulation therein, be discharged from such Service or Labour, but shall be delivered up on Claim of the Party to whom such Service or Labour may be due.

Section 3: New States may be admitted by the Congress into this Union; but no new State shall be formed or erected within the Jurisdiction of any other State; nor any State be formed by the Junction of two or more States, or Parts of States, without the Consent of the Legislatures of the States concerned as well as of the Congress.

The Congress shall have Power to dispose of and make all needful Rules and Regulations respecting the Territory or other Property belonging to the United States; and nothing in this Constitution shall be so construed as to Prejudice any Claims of the United States, or of any particular State.

Section 4: The United States shall guarantee to every State in this Union a Republican Form of Government, and shall protect each of them against Invasion; and on Application of the Legislature, or of the Executive (when the Legislature cannot be convened), against domestic Violence.

Article V

The Congress, whenever two thirds of both Houses shall deem it necessary, shall propose Amendments to this Constitution, or, on the Application of the Legislatures of two thirds of the several States, shall call a Convention for proposing Amendments, which, in either Case, shall be valid to all Intents and Purposes, as Part of this Constitution, when ratified by the Legislatures of three fourths of the several States, or by Conventions in three fourths thereof, as the one or the other Mode of Ratification may be proposed by the Congress; Provided that no

Amendment which may be made prior to the Year One thousand eight hundred and eight shall in any Manner affect the first and fourth Clauses in the Ninth Section of the first Article; and that no State, without its Consent, shall be deprived of its equal Suffrage in the Senate.

Article VI

All Debts contracted and Engagements entered into, before the Adoption of this Constitution, shall be as valid against the United States under this Constitution, as under the Confederation.

This Constitution, and the Laws of the United States which shall be made in Pursuance thereof; and all Treaties made, or which shall be made, under the Authority of the United States, shall be the supreme Law of the Land; and the Judges in every State shall be bound thereby, any Thing in the Constitution or Laws of any State to the Contrary notwithstanding.

The Senators and Representatives before mentioned, and the Members of the several State Legislatures, and all executive and judicial Officers, both of the United States and of the several States, shall be bound by Oath or Affirmation, to support this Constitution; but no religious Test shall ever be required as a Qualification to any Office or public Trust under the United States.

Article VII

The Ratification of the Conventions of nine States, shall be sufficient for the Establishment of this Constitution between the States so ratifying the Same.

The Word, 'the,' being interlined between the seventh and eighth Lines of the first Page, the Word 'Thirty' being partly written on an Erazure in the fifteenth Line of the first Page, The

Words 'is tried' being interlined between the thirty second and thirty third Lines of the first Page and the Word 'the' being interlined between the forty third and forty fourth Lines of the second Page.

Attest William Jackson Secretary

Done in Convention by the Unanimous Consent of the States present the Seventeenth Day of September in the Year of our Lord one thousand seven hundred and Eighty seven and of the Independence of the United States of America the Twelfth In witness whereof We have hereunto subscribed our Names, G. Washington, Presidt and deputy from Virginia

Delaware
Geo: Read
Gunning Bedford jun
John Dickinson
Richard Bassett
Jaco: Broom

Connecticut
Wm. Saml. Johnson
Roger Sherman

Maryland
James McHenry
Dan of St Thos. Jenifer
Danl. Carroll

New Hampshire
John Langdon
Nicholas Gilman

Virginia
John Blair
James Madison Jr.
North Carolina
Wm. Blount
Richd. Dobbs Spaight
Hu Williamson
South CarolinaJ.
Rutledge Charles
Cotesworth Pinckney
Charles Pinckney
Pierce Butler

Georgia
William Few
Abr Baldwin

Massachusetts
Nathaniel Gorham
Rufus King

New York
Alexander Hamilton

New Jersey
Wil: Livingston
David Brearley
Wm. Paterson
Jona: Dayton

Pennsylvania
Benjamin Franklin
Thomas Mifflin
Robt. Morris
Geo. Clymer
Thos. FitzSimons
Jared Ingersoll
James Wilson
Gouv Morris

XIX – Representatives Who Voted for ObamaCare

www.opencongress.org/vote/2010/h/165

Victor Snyder [D,AR–2]
Ann Kirkpatrick [D,AZ–1]
Edward Pastor [D,AZ–4]
Gabrielle Giffords [D,AZ–8]
Harry Mitchell [D,AZ–5]
Raul Grijalva [D,AZ–7]
Barbara Lee [D,CA–9]
Doris Matsui [D,CA–5]
George Miller [D,CA–7]
Lynn Woolsey [D,CA–6]
Michael Thompson [D,CA–1]
Nancy Pelosi [D,CA–8]
Adam Schiff [D,CA–29]
Anna Eshoo [D,CA–14]
Bob Filner [D,CA–51]
Brad Sherman [D,CA–27]
Dennis Cardoza [D,CA–18]
Diane Watson [D,CA–33]
Fortney Stark [D,CA–13]
Grace Napolitano [D,CA–38]
Henry Waxman [D,CA–30]
Howard Berman [D,CA–28]
Jackie Speier [D,CA–12]
Jane Harman [D,CA–36]
Jerry McNerney [D,CA–11]
Jim Costa [D,CA–20]
Joe Baca [D,CA–43]
John Garamendi [D,CA–10]
Judy Chu [D,CA–32]
Laura Richardson [D,CA–37]
Linda Sánchez [D,CA–39]
Lois Capps [D,CA–23]
Loretta Sanchez [D,CA–47]
L. Roybal–Allard [D,CA–34]
Maxine Waters [D,CA–35]
Michael Honda [D,CA–15]
Sam Farr [D,CA–17]
Susan Davis [D,CA–53]
Xavier Becerra [D,CA–31]
Zoe Lofgren [D,CA–16]
Betsy Markey [D,CO–4]
Diana DeGette [D,CO–1]
Ed Perlmutter [D,CO–7]
Jared Polis [D,CO–2]
John Salazar [D,CO–3]
Christopher Murphy [D,CT–5]
James Himes [D,CT–4]
Joe Courtney [D,CT–2]
John Larson [D,CT–1]
Rosa DeLauro [D,CT–3]
Alan Grayson [D,FL–8]
Allen Boyd [D,FL–2]
Corrine Brown [D,FL–3]
Alcee Hastings [D,FL–23]
D. W. Schultz [D,FL–20]
Kathy Castor [D,FL–11]
Kendrick Meek [D,FL–17]
Ron Klein [D,FL–22]
Suzanne Kosmas [D,FL–24]
Henry Johnson [D,GA–4]

John Lewis [D,GA–5]
Sanford Bishop [D,GA–2]
David Scott [D,GA–13]
Mazie Hirono [D,HI–2]
Bruce Braley [D,IA–1]
David Loebsack [D,IA–2]
Leonard Boswell [D,IA–3]
Bobby Rush [D,IL–1]
Danny Davis [D,IL–7]
Janice Schakowsky [D,IL–9]
Jesse Jackson [D,IL–2]
Luis Gutiérrez [D,IL–4]
Melissa Bean [D,IL–8]
Mike Quigley [D,IL–5]
Bill Foster [D,IL–14]
Deborah Halvorson [D,IL–11]
Jerry Costello [D,IL–12]
Phil Hare [D,IL–17]
André Carson [D,IN–7]
Baron Hill [D,IN–9]
Brad Ellsworth [D,IN–8]
Joe Donnelly [D,IN–2]
Peter Visclosky [D,IN–1]
Dennis Moore [D,KS–3]
John Yarmuth [D,KY–3]
Barney Frank [D,MA–4]
Edward Markey [D,MA–7]
James McGovern [D,MA–3]
John Olver [D,MA–1]
John Tierney [D,MA–6]
Michael Capuano [D,MA–8]
Niki Tsongas [D,MA–5]
Richard Neal [D,MA–2]
William Delahunt [D,MA–10]
C. Van Hollen [D,MD–8]
Donna Edwards [D,MD–4]
D. Ruppersberger [D,MD–2]
Elijah Cummings [D,MD–7]
John Sarbanes [D,MD–3]
Steny Hoyer [D,MD–5]
Chellie Pingree [D,ME–1]
Michael Michaud [D,ME–2]
Bart Stupak [D,MI–1]
Dale Kildee [D,MI–5]
Gary Peters [D,MI–9]
Mark Schauer [D,MI–7]
Carolyn Kilpatrick [D,MI–13]
John Conyers [D,MI–14]
John Dingell [D,MI–15]
Sander Levin [D,MI–12]
Betty McCollum [D,MN–4]
James Oberstar [D,MN–8]
Keith Ellison [D,MN–5]
Timothy Walz [D,MN–1]
Emanuel Cleaver [D,MO–5]
Russ Carnahan [D,MO–3]
William Clay [D,MO–1]
Bennie Thompson [D,MS–2]
Bob Etheridge [D,NC–2]
David Price [D,NC–4]
George Butterfield [D,NC–1]
Bradley Miller [D,NC–13]
Melvin Watt [D,NC–12]
Earl Pomeroy [D,ND–0]
Carol Shea–Porter [D,NH–1]
Paul Hodes [D,NH–2]

Frank Pallone [D,NJ–6]
Robert Andrews [D,NJ–1]
Steven Rothman [D,NJ–9]
William Pascrell [D,NJ–8]
Albio Sires [D,NJ–13]
Donald Payne [D,NJ–10]
Rush Holt [D,NJ–12]
Ben Luján [D,NM–3]
Martin Heinrich [D,NM–1]
Dina Titus [D,NV–3]
Shelley Berkley [D,NV–1]
Anthony Weiner [D,NY–9]
Carolyn McCarthy [D,NY–4]
Gary Ackerman [D,NY–5]
Gregory Meeks [D,NY–6]
Jerrold Nadler [D,NY–8]
Joseph Crowley [D,NY–7]
Steve Israel [D,NY–2]
Timothy Bishop [D,NY–1]
Brian Higgins [D,NY–27]
Carolyn Maloney [D,NY–14]
Charles Rangel [D,NY–15]
Daniel Maffei [D,NY–25]
Edolphus Towns [D,NY–10]
Eliot Engel [D,NY–17]
John Hall [D,NY–19]
José Serrano [D,NY–16]
Louise Slaughter [D,NY–28]
Maurice Hinchey [D,NY–22]
Nita Lowey [D,NY–18]
Nydia Velázquez [D,NY–12]
Paul Tonko [D,NY–21]
Scott Murphy [D,NY–20]
William Owens [D,NY–23]
Yvette Clarke [D,NY–11]
Charles Wilson [D,OH–6]
Marcy Kaptur [D,OH–9]
Steve Driehaus [D,OH–1]
Betty Sutton [D,OH–13]
Dennis Kucinich [D,OH–10]
John Boccieri [D,OH–16]
Marcia Fudge [D,OH–11]
Mary Jo Kilroy [D,OH–15]
Timothy Ryan [D,OH–17]
David Wu [D,OR–1]
Earl Blumenauer [D,OR–3]
Kurt Schrader [D,OR–5]
Peter DeFazio [D,OR–4]
Chaka Fattah [D,PA–2]
Joe Sestak [D,PA–7]
K. Dahlkemper [D,PA–3]
Patrick Murphy [D,PA–8]
Robert Brady [D,PA–1]
Allyson Schwartz [D,PA–13]
Christopher Carney [D,PA–10]
Michael Doyle [D,PA–14]
Paul Kanjorski [D,PA–11]
James Langevin [D,RI–2]
Patrick Kennedy [D,RI–1]
James Clyburn [D,SC–6]
John Spratt [D,SC–5]
Barton Gordon [D,TN–6]
Jim Cooper [D,TN–5]
Steve Cohen [D,TN–9]
Al Green [D,TX–9]
Charles Gonzalez [D,TX–20]

Ciro Rodriguez [D,TX–23]
Eddie Johnson [D,TX–30]
Henry Cuellar [D,TX–28]
Lloyd Doggett [D,TX–25]
Raymond Green [D,TX–29]
Rubén Hinojosa [D,TX–15]
Sheila Jackson–Lee [D,TX–18]
Silvestre Reyes [D,TX–16]
Solomon Ortiz [D,TX–27]
James Moran [D,VA–8]
Robert Scott [D,VA–3]
Thomas Perriello [D,VA–5]
Gerald Connolly [D,VA–11]
Peter Welch [D,VT–0]
Adam Smith [D,WA–9]
Brian Baird [D,WA–3]
James McDermott [D,WA–7]
Jay Inslee [D,WA–1]
Norman Dicks [D,WA–6]
Rick Larsen [D,WA–2]
David Obey [D,WI–7]
Gwen Moore [D,WI–4]
Ronald Kind [D,WI–3]
Steve Kagen [D,WI–8]
Tammy Baldwin [D,WI–2]
Alan Mollohan [D,WV–1]
Nick Rahall [D,WV–3]

Sources

Angle, Jim, *IRS Targets Taxpayers Hiding Income in Offshore Accounts,* FoxNews.com, April 20, 2010........................118

Armey, Dick, *Out of Control,* American Spectator, April 2010100

Associated Press, *Black Tea Party Activists Called Traitors,* April 06, 2010..107

Associated Press, *Obama Criticizes Virginia Governor for Slavery Omission in Confederacy Month Proclamation,* April 09, 2010108

Associated Press, *Poll: Trust in Big Government Near Historic Low, April 19, 2010*..129

Barone, Michael, *Hold the VAT — Taxpayers May Prefer Spending Cuts,* Real Clear Politic, April 26, 2010............................98

Barone, Michael, *ObamaCare and the Supreme Court,* Real Clear Politics, April 12, 2010...111

Barone, Michael, *Tea Partiers Fight Culture of Dependence,* Real Clear Politics, *April 19, 2010*....................................54, 126

Barone, Michael, *U.S. Bond AAA Rating,* Real Clear Politics, March 25, 2010...122

Bernstein, Sharon, *Happy Meal toys could be banned in Santa Clara County,* Los Angeles Times, April 27, 2010..................103

Bowman, Karlyn, Senior fellow American Enterprise Institute, *Liar, Liar,* Forbes, April 5, 2010.......................................129

Caldwell, Christopher, *Don't expect real reform from the Wall Street Democrats,* Weekly Standard, May 10, 2010..................139

Camia, Catalina, and Schouten, Fredreka, *Rep. Rangel says he'll step down for now as Ways and Means chairman,* USA Today, March 3, 2010..141

Cohen, Richard, *Were Liberals Wrong on Crime?,* Real Clear Politics, June 2, 2010 128

Cuccinelli, Virginia Attorney General Kenneth T., *Unconstitutional Mandate,* April 9, 2010 110

Emery, Noemie, *Media still clueless about Tea Parties,* Washington Examiner, April 28, 2010 121

FoxNews.com, *Ex–Official Accuses Justice Department of Racial Bias in Black Panther Case, July 06, 2010* 105

FoxNews.com, *Mississippi Gov. Barbour Backs McDonnell,* April 11, 2010 108

Friedman, Thomas L., *Start–Ups, Not Bailouts,* New York Times, April 3, 2010 98

Gingrich, *Newt, To Save America: Stopping Obama's Secular–Socialist Machine, 2010*...63, 122

Goldberg, Jonah, *Taxes,* USAToday, April 5, 2010 116

Gordon, John Steele, *The Global Reform Dodge,* CommentaryMagazine.com, May 03, 2010..................135

Hanson, Victor Davis, *Our American Catharsis,* National Review, April 9, 2010 113

Kramer, Marcia, *House Committee To Expand Rangel Investigation,* CBS News, October 9, 2009 140

Kuhn, David Paul, *Exit polls: How Obama Won,* Politico, November 5, 2008 106

Levin, Yuval, *Finding Out What's In It,* National Review, May 06, 2010 135

Lochhead, Carolyn, *National debt seen heading for crisis level,* San Francisco Chronicle, April 5, 2010 123

Mott, Dr. Jonathan, *A Flexible Document,* Thenation.com 152

Mott, Dr. Jonathan, *A Republican Form of Government,* Thenation.com 59

Nakashima, Ellen and Kane, Paul, *Dozens in Congress under ethics inquiry,* Washington Post, October 30, 2009.................. 141

O'Reilly, Bill, *Culture Warrior, 2007*.................................... 63

Pence, Mike, and Rodgers, Cathy McMorris, *We're bailing out Greece, But U.S. taxpayers shouldn't be,* New York Post, May 8, 2010.. 123

Samuelson, Robert, *The Poisonous Politics of Self–Esteem,* Washington Post, April 4, 2010 101

Sowell, Thomas, *Race and Politics,* Real Clear Politics, April 6, 2010.. 106

Steenhuysen, Julie, *FDA should regulate salt, panel says,* Reuters, April 20, 2010 112

Stossel, John, *Myths About Capitalism,* Real Clear Politics, April 21, 2010 127

Stossel, John, *What am I,* Real Clear Politics, April 7, 2010126

Superville, Darlene, *'Go for it,' Obama tells GOP on health repeal,* Washington Times, March 25, 2010 143

Thomma, Steven, *Obama energy official has ties to firms that stand to benefit,* McClatchy Newspapers, April 26, 2010............ 142

Wallison, Peter J, *Fannie and Freddie Amnesia,* Wall Street Journal, April 20, 2010 137

Winter, Jana, *Tea Partiers Seek 'Teachable Moment,' Not Oregon Teacher's Job,* FoxNews.com, April 20, 2010.................... 54

York, Byron, *Obama's trillions dwarf Bush's 'dangerous' spending,* Washington Examiner, February 24, 2009 125

Index

www.ingramcontent.com/pod-product-compliance
Lightning Source LLC
Chambersburg PA
CBHW060841280326
41934CB00007B/867

9780615380445